FOOTPRINTS THROUGH THE STORM

By Stacie Adams

PRESS

Table of Contents

ॐॐ

Introduction

❦

L ike the very familiar poem "Footprints in the Sand" describes how the Lord carried a person during their lowest moments, "Footprints through the Storm" implies how our Heavenly Father carries us through tragedies and lends us His strength even though we may never see the evidence of His footprints to remind us that it was His doing that preserved our lives from utter despair.

This book is actually a collection of emails written over a four-year period to an ever-growing list of friends and supporters. What these emails delivered was a blow-by-blow description of both the encouraging and the tragic events that touched the lives of me and my family as they happened during that time; much like a sports announcer might report the live action as it occurs on a football or baseball field. Many of the e-mails were for my own therapy as they helped me stay in check with reality, as well as minister to our friends that had so lovingly prayed for us. Each e-mail represents the sum of my thoughts and emotions in that moment in time without knowledge or concern for the future.

In February of 2010 the Lord told me to gather up all of the emails that I could find and compile them into this book. I have never even dreamed of writing a book, so when you laugh, smile, cry, get angry or are inspired, remember I am just the keyboard operator.

We did nothing to contribute to the tragedies that occurred in our lives, but we did traverse storms in a manner that honored our Creator.

My prayer is that many people will be inspired to walk through the storms in their lives with courage, dignity and unstoppable faith. Every human being on this planet goes through a storm at some point in their lives, maybe even multiple times. Those storms are going to hurt like crazy, but there is joy in the morning if you know the secret.

"Life isn't about waiting for the storm to pass. It's about learning to dance in the rain." ~Pat Landon

"The purpose of life is a life of purpose." ~ Robert Byrne

Chapter 1

September 9, 2006
Subject: Six Million Dollar Man

Hi Everyone,

This is just a quick note to let you know that Larry's total knee replacements went off without a hitch and that he is doing very well. You may call him directly in his room. He has a nerve blocking line in each of his thighs and a morphine push every six minutes but he is still pretty coherent all the same.

Joyfully His,
Stacie

Sept. 16, 2006

Subject: Six Million Dollar Man at Home

Hi Everybody,

Well, I brought the Six Million Dollar Man home yesterday and outside of being a twelve on a pain scale of ten he is way ahead of schedule in his healing process.

Thank you for all the thoughtfulness, kindness and love that you have blessed us with in the past eight days. It is awesome and humbling to realize what truly sweet friends we have.

We love you all,
Stacie & Larry

July 13, 2007
Subject: About Larry

Hello Everyone,

Larry was admitted to the Portsmouth Naval Hospital yesterday for leukemia. He is in a private room and can have visitors 24/7. There is a private phone line next to his bed so you are welcome to call.
Chemo therapy will start as soon as he is strong enough. We covet your prayers in faith for his miraculous healing.

Joyfully His,
Stacie & Larry

July 15, 2007
Subject: Update on Larry

Hello Everyone,

Larry has had every kind of poke, stab and prod imaginable, and he keeps cracking jokes to perk up the spirits of everyone with whom he comes into contact. Together we made tears well up in the eyes of his internal medicine doctor when we shared our faith that God has already healed him and that to quote Larry, "I am only here as a training tool for all of you to practice medicine." The diagnosis is leukemia. He is receiving blood transfusions and has a permanent IV or "pic" installed for the purpose of chemotherapy, which I suppose will begin next week after the bone biopsy results are analyzed. The best case scenario from the oncologist, internal medicine and cardiac doctors are all very bleak at best and they expect Larry to be there for at least the next month.

Now for the good news: Larry and I fully expect God to heal him and "We ain't sceeerd!"

I love you,
Stacie

July 16, 2007
Subject: About Larry

Hello Everyone,

I want to thank all of you for the fabulous outpouring of prayer, phone calls, cards and e-mail. I have not been able to answer all of your e-mails yet, but I will.

Larry had a very grueling day with two different kinds of stress tests, so he was quite exhausted this afternoon and evening.

Now for some awesome news: First, Larry is strong enough to receive the chemo, second he has a kind of leukemia that responds well to chemo and has between a 50 to 70 percent recovery rate and thirdly he starts chemotherapy tomorrow morning (July 17).

Larry's faith is strong and we are both very grateful for the love, compassion and healing of our Lord, Jesus Christ. We simply cannot verbally express how vital each one of your prayers are to the continued miraculous healing taking place in Larry's body.

Prayers that aren't prayed will never be answered! "Yet you do not have because you do not ask." ~ Jesus. So be encouraged to pray, knowing that your Heavenly Father yearns to bless His children.

We love you guys sooooooooooo much!

Joyfully His,
Larry & Stacie

July 18, 2007
Subject: First Dose

Hi Everyone,

Yesterday Larry received his first installment of chemotherapy and it went smoothly. He is receiving seven days of continuous medicine, but the first three days are a closely monitored injection into the permanently installed IV "pic" line that goes straight to his heart.

His attitude is awesome and inspiring to everyone that he comes into contact with. Thank you for continuing to lift us up in prayer.

Joyfully His,
Larry & Stacie

Thursday, July 19, 2007
Subject: Three Days of Chemo

Hi Everyone,

Well, today is day three of chemo for Larry ɛ doing great! I stayed the night with him last night thinking that he might be able to sleep better knowing that I was right there. I was wrong. So not only is he tired from the treatments, but he is also lacking in sleep.

Just as when he was recovering from the dual knee replacement surgery, the pain medications (I think it is the morphine) are making him as emotional as a woman with menopause.

Out of every adversity comes the seed of equal or greater opportunity. Larry has not been in communication with his youngest son in years. He is going to be so thrilled (beyond comprehension) this afternoon when I take him an e-mail and pictures of his daughter-in-law and granddaughter that Larry never knew existed until today and only because of this life changing situation.

Rejoice in the Lord always, again I say rejoice! Let your gentle spirit be known to all men. The Lord is near. Be anxious for nothing, but in everything by prayer and supplication with thanksgiving let your requests be made known to God. And the peace of God, which surpasses all comprehension, will guard your hearts and your minds in Christ Jesus. Finally, my dear friends, whatever is true, whatever is honorable, whatever is right, whatever is pure, whatever is lovely, whatever is admirable, if there is any excellent or praiseworthy, think only about these things. (Philippians 4:4-8)

Thank you for all of your love and prayers.

Joyfully His,
Larry & Stacie

July 20, 2007
Subject: How Chemo Works

Hi Everyone,

Today has been another great one here on planet Earth. Larry is responding very well to having the abnormal and mutated cells in his body virtually exploded. Someone asked me today to explain what is happening with the chemo, so I thought it might be helpful to share the explanation this evening.

Larry is receiving two radioactive drugs that specifically target bone marrow and abnormal cells found in the blood. The chemo is literally causing the bad cells to explode so they can be expelled from his body. You know how sometimes your computer will slow down or start acting funny and you have to reboot it? Well Larry's bone marrow started producing garbled cells so the chemo is destroying the bad cells and stunning the bone marrow, so when it starts producing blood again, it will produce the right stuff.

Larry received two pints of whole blood today as well as a bag of platelets. Again, part of the chemo process is designed to wipe out the bad stuff so that after stunning the bone marrow, it spontaneously resets to the previous standards. In the process, blood augmentation and supplementation is required to maintain life sustaining parameters.

Now all of this is very fascinating information but the truth is: Jesus is the Great Physician, and Larry's body was healed two thousand years ago. Our redemption is complete: spirit, soul and body.

Joyfully His,
Larry & Stacie

July 21-23, 2007
Subject: Decisions to Make

Hi Everyone,

As you may have guessed, Larry and I are engaging in the process of reviewing our affairs to ensure that they are really in compliance with our priorities. It has been six years since we updated our wills. I had the opportunity to share with our son Matthew the decision that my siblings and I were forced to make concerning my mother's death, and how and why we arrived at that conclusion 16 years ago. Knowing what I know now I don't think we would have given up so soon. Every life is precious and sacred. If we have the science and technology to heal and save lives then not to use it is a waste.

Years before my mother died, she did something extremely wise. She gave each one of us siblings what she wanted us to have and asked us if there was anything special of hers that we desired. This exercise caused us to think about our own mortality and provided a framework for expressing our deepest thoughts and feelings. So now Larry and I are engaging in the same process. It's truly amazing how such a discussion can deepen the love and relationship within a family.

A few years before my father's death, he asked me to make sure that if he died in Alaska that we would not try to bury his body in Nevada next to mom and his four year old grandson. I was a little overwhelmed to be entrusted with such responsibility but my father quickly reminded me that I was just disposing of his earth suit not the real him who is an eternal spirit.

To some of you this kind of talk may seem morbid, but I assure you that just like King Hezekiah, Larry has been granted more time in order to fulfill God's destiny for his life.

Joyfully His,
Larry & Stacie

July 24, 2007
Subject: A Typical Day

Yesterday, Larry had his first "typical" day for chemotherapy which included some nausea but no vomiting. The good news is that he has not had any until now, and his white blood cell count is at an all-time low which is what they were trying to accomplish. So for now we are asking for people not to visit until his immune system recovers. Larry loves the phone calls though, so please keep them coming.

Joyfully His,
Larry & Stacie

August 6, 2007
Subject: Update on Larry's Progress

Hi Everyone,

I know that it has been at least a week since my last update, and some of you have called to see if this is bad news. Fortunately the answer to that is a resounding "no." It is just the contrary. Larry is progressing just as they expected him to, and he is doing everything that they have asked him to do. He remains in good spirits although the chemo and the expected results were harsh. His white blood cell count is back up so that he feels comfortable having visitors again, so....... come on down!

Larry's hair was falling out in rapid order this morning so he shaved his head. Even though it is so un-Larry-like to have a shaved head, it doesn't look bad. Besides, now he is right in style with all of the other manly men that don't have time for "no stinking hair!" Oh, also while his blood count was very low, his eyes dried out and itched, causing him to rub them a lot, which caused bruising. As a result, he kind of looks like Captain Jack Sparrow. Between the shaved head and the eyeliner effect, it is a very different look for him, but I think he is cuter than ever.

Larry and I have been endeavoring to implement steps number eight and nine of the twelve step AA program this week. Step eight: Make a list of people we have harmed, and been willing to make amends to them all. Step nine: Make direct amends to such people wherever possible, except when to do so would injure them or others. I intend to keep my life free of the clutter of unforgiveness and strife. Jesus said, " Therefore if you are presenting your offering at the altar, and there remember that your brother has something against you, leave your offering there before the altar and go; first be reconciled to your brother, and then come and present your offering."

Even if I am in the right, it will not aid in good communication or the furtherance of a relationship to harbor ill will. So I am quick to apologize because I refuse to let pride rob me of the joy of friendship. (We have been able to put this into practice twice in the past week.) You know it is just like the devil to find people to say horrible things to you when you are involved in challenging circumstances.

We cannot thank you enough for your continued prayers and love.

Joyfully His,
Larry & Stacie

August 13, 2007
Subject: Going Home—For Awhile

Hello Everyone,

Well surprise! Larry got to come home today for some rest and relaxation before returning next Monday for the second round of chemotherapy.

Visitors are welcome with a couple of precautions. First, please call before coming over. Secondly, we need to limit Larry's close contact with children.

We thank each of you for your thoughts, prayers, cards and gifts. Your outpouring of affection has made this soooooo much easier to deal with. We love you all.

Joyfully His,
Larry & Stacie

August 20, 2007
Subject: Follow-Up Biopsy

Hi Everyone,

Thursday, the 16th of August, we went for a follow up bone marrow biopsy for which we will not know the result for a few more days. What we did find out is that one of Larry's liver enzymes is still elevated, so we had to postpone the second cycle of his chemotherapy (that was supposed to start today) until this coming Thursday.

Two things I keep repeating: God is in control and He never gives us more than We can handle. The reason that I capitalized "We" is that we can only handle these challenges because He is our God.

My dear friend and wise matriarch of a huge family recently reminded me of the following truth: "Where there is no fight - there can be no victory!" And we are more than conquerors through Christ Jesus who strengthens us.

Joyfully His,
Larry & Stacie

August 23, 2007
Subject: Second Round of Chemo

Hi Everyone,

We got up extra early this morning to get to the hospital before the traffic got bad and so we could get two chemo treatments in today as planned. But guess what? Larry's liver function enzymes were still elevated. So after a few hours of deliberation, the doctor decided to postpone cycle two of the chemotherapy until Monday, August 27th. That means that Larry will actually be in attendance at Matthew's wedding this Sunday the 26th. *Yeeeee - Haaaaah!*

One of the nurses in the Oncology Ward gave us a book called "The Four Things That Matter Most," by Ira Byock, M.D. It's a book about living and completing relationships before we die. He uses short story-style excerpts of his clinical experiences with people from all walks of life to show how they used their impending deaths to bless, empower and heal the people that they loved. The author does a great job of sharing how well we can live our lives, improve our relationships and have our deaths be a wonderful transition rather than a gut wrenching grieving process.

May God continue to bless each of you abundantly.

Joyfully His,
Larry & Stacie

August 28, 2007
Subject: Something to Celebrate

Hi Everyone,

Wow, has this week been a whirlwind of excitement!

You may recall that Larry's bilirubin was elevated, which was the reason for postponing the second cycle of chemo two times. But God has a way of working everything out in His timing for our good. Matthew and Elaine got married on Sunday in a beautiful ceremony on the shore of the Intracoastal Waterway. Although we were experiencing a heat wave, the wedding was perfect and immediately after the ceremony it started to rain and cooled down 20 degrees. As a result, the reception was perfect. Oh, the theme of the wedding was Tropical/Luau and everyone was dressed happily casual.

Early yesterday morning Larry went back into the hospital to start his chemo and should be back home on Saturday after receiving six treatments. He will come home to recover for about three weeks and then report back for round three of chemo. Visitors are always welcome. Please send any cards to our home address so that he can receive them in a timely manner.

Our Pastor often states that at any given moment, each of us is either going into a storm, are in the middle of a storm or coming out of one in our lives. Life is not static (if it is you are dying), but quite fluid. I read a book called "Storms of Perfection" by Andy Andrews that is a collection of stories about famous people and the struggles that they endured to get where they are now. They all had the following in common: perseverance, courage and faith. Their struggles or storms defined them and caused them to fulfill their destiny. Larry and I are walking THROUGH the valley of the shadow of death. Although this is a storm, it is also a mountaintop experience at the same time. Our prayers and conversations with God have more efficacy and have created a more intimate relationship with Him than ever before! WE AIN'T SCEEEEEEEERD!!! Not because we are so special, but because our Creator and His only begotten Son, Jesus, are.

The prayers of the saints are a precious fragrance in the nostrils of God, especially when offered for unselfish reasons.

Joyfully His,
Larry & Stacie

September 1, 2007
Subject: Back Home

Hi Everyone,

Yes, it is true; Larry is back home once again after round two of chemotherapy. He feels absolutely great, and he looks wonderful also.

Healthy visitors are welcome, but if you are not feeling your best please postpone your visit since Larry's immune system is compromised as a result of the chemo. He will not be able to have any fresh or dried fruits or vegetables and no bakery or cream filled items either. And worst of all for Larry, no buffet dinners! All of these measures are designed to limit the introduction of bacteria to his body. Oh, it is not a good idea for him to hang around with children either until all of his treatments are complete, which may stretch into December.

Your prayers have made a world of difference and we covet your continued diligence.

Joyfully His,
Larry & Stacie

September 6, 2007
Subject: Running Low

Hi Everyone,

We saw the doctor today and tomorrow Larry will go to the hospital and receive two pints of whole blood and a pint of platelets. Does that conjure up visions of being nearly two quarts low on oil?

The low blood counts and need for transfusions are normal in patients receiving chemotherapy, so this is nothing to be alarmed about. The infusions should take about seven hours, and I will bring him home when he is finished.

Thank you again for all of your diligence in prayer and love toward us.

Joyfully His,
Larry & Stacie

September 9, 2007
Subject: Our Church

Hey Everyone,

Our church is a modern day manifestation of the early church depicted in the book of Acts in their desire to come to the rescue of a brother in need. It started when Larry was initially hospitalized for 30 days when a friend from the church came and installed a doggie door into the garage for my former little couch potato dogs so I did not have to come home to any surprises. Then there was the possibility that we had some black mold in the walls of one of our bathrooms and the doctor said that there was no way that he could let Larry come home if there was even the remote possibility of it in the house, because the consequences would be devastating in Larry's weakened condition.

A ministry in our church called the Carpenter's Hammer (all volunteers) donated their time and talent to completely rip out the entire exterior wall and rebuild it from the ground up. Remember that when we bought this house it had been a rental for at least 10 years and one of the conditions of purchase was NOT to get an inspection. So although this project was on our "to-do" list, it was not going to get accomplished for at least another year.

What a Godsend to have our church family come to our rescue in our darkest hour.

We pray that each of you develop relationships with people who will love you and come save the day in your time of need just like Larry and I have been so fortunate to have.

Joyfully His,
Larry & Stacie

September 16, 2007
Subject: Grateful

Hi Everyone,

Here we are on a lovely, lazy Sunday afternoon, just counting our blessings and being grateful for all of the wonderful people that God has put into our lives—people who have lifted us up in prayer and loved on us and provided us with a constant source of encouragement. We are overwhelmed with the generosity and compassion and caring that has been shown toward us! The experience has been most humbling as well as magnificently beautiful. Larry and I can truly say that we are observing the body of Christ in action ministering to us as well as others in a time of great need.

It has been 10 days since I last e-mailed so let me fill you in on what is going on with Larry. Last Thursday Larry received his weekly blood tests, which verified that he is still neutropenic (high white count, low red count and susceptible to germs). Of course, that is exactly where they expect him to be right now. He is feeling pretty good, and he is actually driving a little bit, which is great for his spirits.

Larry has received literally hundreds of cards and notes that continually serve to reassure him how special and loved he is and he dearly appreciates them. I can't tell you how many times I have failed to drop someone a note thinking that it would be inconsequential, but now I know that cards are like laughter; they are medicine to the soul! Oh yes and please do not let me fail to mention the visits and the benevolence of care packages, goodies and food. Larry did not marry me for my cooking abilities but at least I have succeeded in putting some weight back on him recently.

Joyfully His,
Larry & Stacie

September 24, 2007
Subject: Round Two

Hi Everyone,

Larry checked into the hospital today to receive round two of four scheduled chemotherapy cycles. The doctor is very excited about Larry's progress and his exceptional tolerance to the chemo. Of course, we all know that is because he is already healed by the Healer Himself as a result of intercessory prayer. (I cannot thank you enough)

Larry is located in the same room as before with the same phone number, so please do not hesitate to call or visit! Oh, he will be coming home again on Saturday.

Joyfully His,
Larry & Stacie

September 27, 2007
Subject: 15 Years of Adventure

Hi Everyone,

Well today was a chemo day for Larry, but he also received two packs of whole blood so he is in the pink so to speak again. The fact that he has not had any stomach problems is a testimony to his healing.

Today marked 15 years since I left the Army. I can't believe how fast that went! I am still experiencing a lot of adventures and enjoying them even more. This may sound crazy, but I don't mind challenging circumstances in my life because it gives me a chance to watch my heavenly Father at work. Through Larry's dual knee replacement a year ago and this illness, the Lord has skillfully led me through literally hundreds of mine field situations. I cannot adequately express how grateful I am for my awesome God coming to the rescue in every tiny situation in our life. His promises are true, and we are getting the opportunity to prove them first hand.

Father, we ask You to bless our friends, relatives and those whom we care deeply for who are reading this right now. Show them a new revelation of your love and power. Holy Spirit, we ask You to minister to their spirit at this very moment. Where there is pain, give them your peace and mercy. Where there is self-doubt, release a renewed confidence through your grace. Where there is need, we ask You to fulfill their needs. Bless their homes, families, finances, their goings and their comings. In Jesus' precious name. Amen.

Thank you for your love, support and continued PRAYERS.

Joyfully His,
Larry & Stacie

October 10, 2007
Subject: Testimony

Hi Everyone,

Yes, I know that it has been a long time since you received a "Larry Update," but I think reading the testimony he delivered at church tonight is worth the wait.

LARRY'S TESTIMONY

Hello, my name is Larry Adams, and I have been asked to share my testimony about how God has sustained me and my family. I have been the recipient of God's healing twice. The first was a rapid recovery from bilateral knee replacement in September of 2006. The second is my healing from the most aggressive and dangerous type of blood cancer; called acute myelogenous leukemia, for which I was hospitalized on July 12th this year.

God has sustained Stacie and I through all of these challenges in numerous ways.

We have been blessed by having a wonderful God that loves us and a Bible believing and teaching church with a staff that is fantastic.

God sustains us through our Sunday School Class by providing support in a number of ways. We always have great fellowship in or outside of class. They have become our best friends and family. God has used them to sustain us and minister to us through food, phone calls, visits both at home or in the hospital, cards and notes of encouragement and most importantly prayers of faith!!!!

God sustained me through the sweet hand-made cards of preschoolers from the church. I plastered them all over the walls of my hospital room and used them to minister to the hearts of the hospital staff.

God has sustained us by providing loyal friends and family and their churches all over the world to faithfully uplift us in prayer and to intercede on our behalf.

God sustained my physical household by sending twelve Christian brothers to my rescue to finish the projects that I had started. I cannot begin to tell you how much these efforts meant to me, and how grateful I am that our church and its members are so ready to minister to those in need.

God sustained me during both recoveries by planting a hunger in me for His Word. God put a desire in me to spend more time with Him. I watched TV ministries about three to four hours per day. I started writing healing scriptures in my notebook. My rehab from knee surgery allowed me to get into the Bible like I had never done before. Oh, I had read the entire Bible all the way through several times and each time I would find something I hadn't noticed before. But during this time I was doing a more meaningful and comprehensive study of God's word in such a way as to discover all that He has in store for me and also for all of His children.

God has supernaturally sustained us financially so that our income actually increased while I have been out of work.

All of the study and writing and spending time in the Bible and with God following my knee rehabilitation turned out to be an unexpected asset when I was diagnosed with leukemia. There is no correlation between the knee replacement surgery and the leukemia, it just happened.

The emergency room doctor who broke the news to us about the cancer took it harder than we did. He was choked up and teary eyed. I will admit that it was quite a blow, but I immediately turned to Stacie and said to her, "I am coming in healed, and I am going out of here healed." We had to pull ourselves together because fear is lack of faith in God as our provider and protector and healer. Fear and faith cannot exist in the same heart at the same time, so we had to start right then speaking God's word about being healed, calling those things that are not as though they are. By Jesus' stripes I am healed!!!!!!

We honored and praised God with our words and with our faith, and God has done such wonderful things for me. My doctors are totally amazed and even the ones that are not Christians are starting to believe. Not only did I use my mouth to confess healing scriptures, but I also had a CD player going night and day with healing scriptures or praise and worship music, so that I was constantly hearing and saying God's words for me from Him.

God's hand was on us in a very strong way from the very start of the cancer ordeal. When I was admitted to the hospital several of my organs were extremely enlarged. My liver and spleen were so enlarged that my lungs and heart were being compressed, and I was very short of breath. I was literally at death's door. Because of the treacherous and aggressive nature of this type of leukemia, I would be in heaven with Jesus if I had delayed even an hour or two before going to the hospital. God is soooooo good!!!

When we started the chemotherapy, I weighed 192 pounds, which over the next 31 days dropped down to 171 pounds. The weight loss can be dangerous, because you do not have the strength to withstand the chemo. However, God protected and sustained me, and I never once felt any nausea or vomiting that makes the chemo treatment so rough. In fact, as of the last two cycles of inpatient week-long chemotherapy sessions, I have actually gained weight.

Because I have had such favor from God, my doctor wants me to undergo two more week-long treatments to totally get rid of all traces of the cancer. Normally, someone my age is not able to tolerate more than the two cycles that I have already had. He may not be completely aware of the fact that Jesus healed me years ago, but I am there for all the medical staff to practice on. I am there so they can brush up on their procedures for those patients who come in that are not already healed.

I had read all the scriptures about Jesus dying on the cross and taking all our sins upon his body so that if we believed in Him, that He was born of a virgin, died on the cross and on the third day rose from the dead, we could be saved and have eternal life in heaven with Him. That by itself is a pretty awesome deal, but when we read and understand all that God has for us it becomes even better.

Surely He has borne our grief, and carried our sorrows, yet we esteemed Him stricken, smitten by God, and afflicted, but He was wounded for our transgressions, He was bruised for our iniquities, the chastisement of our peace was upon Him and by His stripes we are healed. (Isaiah 53: 4-5) Yes, by His stripes we are healed. It is already done. The same faith that saves you from sin has healed your body. But in my studies I read that we have to be active with our faith and spend time with God in prayer and in His word. Just as God wanted to bless His people, Israel, in the Old Testament, the same is available today for us under the New Covenant.

God sustained us through these months by His grace and mercy as well as His word, which greatly enhanced my knowledge of His perfect will for His children.

God has not only sustained us spirit, soul and body over these past 13 months, but he has also used us in a mighty way to physically and financially sustain, uplift, encourage and inspire others to be all that God has designed and destined them to be.

(Larry was given the opportunity to read the above testimony to the entire church congregation on Wednesday, October 10, 2007.)

Joyfully His,
Larry & Stacie

October 22, 2007
Subject: Round Four

Hi Everybody,

Larry went into the hospital today for round four of high dose chemo so he will only have one more cycle after this one. He has been tolerating the chemo so well that his doctor decided to put him through the maximum five cycles.

Okay, here is the drill. Larry can have calls 24/7, because he has a private line right next to his bed. If you would like to send him a card the house address is the most expedient.

When I was about seven years old a very wise and matronly neighbor lady sat me down and explained something very profound.

"Stacie, when you are very old and near the end of your life, you will sit in a rocking chair looking back on your life and evaluate it, the only regrets that you will experience are those things that you failed to do. Oh, I am sure you will have plenty of embarrassing memories of things that you will wish you had not done, but they will not cause you regret. No, the things that you will truly regret are the things that you wanted to do but were too scared or selfish or pressured into not doing them."

She went on to explain how she had wanted to join the Women's Army Corp during WWI, but her family and friends had talked her out of it. By the time WWII broke out she was married, so there was no way to join the WAC. She made me promise her that I would always follow my dreams no matter how strange they seemed to others.

I believe that was the seed—planted by that wonderful lady that day—that caused me to grow up and join the Army just after the WACs were disbanded.

I currently have another very wise matronly neighbor who recently explained to me that, "Where there is NO BATTLE there can be NO VICTORY where God is concerned. And it is IMPOSSIBLE to please God WITHOUT FAITH!"

Larry's illness has caused us to search our lives to see what we have left undone or foolishly put off thinking that we still have lots of time. This challenge has been a wakeup call to do battle in the unseen realm against God's enemies and to truly trust Him for everything!

It is our sincere prayer that each of you would look at our circumstances and use it to propel you to follow your dreams now, with no regrets, and faithfully trust God who has put that dream in your heart.

Joyfully His,
Larry & Stacie

October 29, 2007
Subject: Larry in ICU

Larry's heart stopped so that he passed out this afternoon in our kitchen and I gave him CPR until the paramedics arrived. We do not know the cause and he has not gained consciousness yet. He is currently very heavily sedated.

Stacie

October 30, 2007
Subject: A Few Minutes in Heaven

Hi Everyone,

Larry spent a few minutes with Jesus in Heaven yesterday. Although protocol dictates that only two shocks with the defibrillator paddles be administered, I believe it was the power of faith-filled prayer that provoked the paramedics to give Larry the third shock that finally restarted his heart.

I dialed 911 on the run to Sandy's, my prayer warrior neighbor, giving my address while simultaneously telling Sandy to come quick. She was able to stand out front praying and bring in the rescue crew, as the dispatcher instructed me on the new rules for CPR and listened to me count as she coached over the phone.

We now have yet another testimony as to the absolute power of prayer. Although we don't know what caused Larry's heart to stop him in his tracks ... we do know that it was not a stroke and it was not a heart attack or a side effect of the chemotherapy. So there is no damage to his heart or brain, and I am grateful that he went down right in the kitchen just three feet from me where I was able to help him to the floor without severe trauma. I am also grateful that he was not by himself in the garage where he planned to be 10 minutes later, or when he was driving us home just 20 minutes earlier. I am grateful for the mercy of a great God that continues to sustain my dear sweet husband.

Currently, all of Larry's sedatives have been turned off and although he is still on the ventilator, he is breathing on his own. I am on watch so that when he wakes up he doesn't rip all of the tubes out of his mouth! As soon as he wakes they will take all the tubes out. However, he could sleep for another 20 hours as a result of the tremendous workout he had yesterday, which has left him totally exhausted.

I have included some scriptures concerning fear and love that explain where our power comes from. Please invoke them as you pray for us.

"There is no fear in love. But perfect love casts out fear, because fear has to do with punishment. The one who fears is not made perfect in love." (1 John 4:18)

"For God did not give us a spirit of timidity (fear), but a spirit of power, love and of a sound mind." (2 Timothy 1:7)

Thank you all once again for your faith filled diligent prayers.

Joyfully His,
Larry & Stacie

October 31, 2007
Subject: Waiting

Hi Everyone,

Well to quote our pastor, "Larry is doing his impression of Rip Van Winkle!"

The neurologist ran more tests today and said that most of Larry's functions look pretty good. They did an EEG today as well and discovered NO seizure activity! All of Larry's vitals and systems remain strong. He did receive platelets today as a normal course of the down swing of the chemo cycle. He is also receiving some good snacks through a feeding tube that should help him regain his strength.

Please pray that he wakes up tomorrow and that he has a supernaturally speedy recovery.

Joyfully His,
Larry & Stacie

November 1, 2007
Subject: An Eventful Day

Hi Everyone,

God has a plan, and Larry and I are very much a part of it. Our job is to believe that God will do His job and fulfill all of His promises. *I (God) will NEVER leave you or forsake you. The Lord is my helper; I will not be afraid.* (Hebrews 13:5, 6)

Well, today was very eventful. Larry opened his eyes and blinked numerous times and all of his vitals remain good. (This is not actually considered awake.) He received a pint of whole blood and a new PIC line in his right arm and the removal of the PIC line in his left arm. (I don't know what the acronym stands for but it is an IV that goes all the way up his arm nearly into his heart.) He also breathed while on the ventilator for two hours completely on his own. Even in the ventilator assisted mode, he initiates about three breaths a minute on his own.

It seems to be a mystery why he is still sleeping, but patience is a fruit of the Spirit that requires exercise just like working any other muscle.

Larry continues to be a training tool for all of these people to learn where true healing comes from. To quote Larry, "I am coming in healed and I am going out healed."

Joyfully His,
Larry & Stacie

November 4, 2007
Subject: Trust in God

Hello Everyone,

I need to share some decisions with you that Larry and I agreed upon when we found out that he had leukemia.

Due to our faith in God and our belief in the sanctity of life, we decided to walk through ANY circumstance that might happen with faith and courage. We agreed that only fearful cowards or ignorantly prideful fools make provisions to quit either by their own hand or a termination clause in a living will or advance directive. This is strictly our personal thought process, and it is not meant to hurt anyone's feelings.

We chose to completely sell out to God and trust Him lock stock and barrel with our lives. We do not want to be lukewarm, withholding any part of ourselves from being used to accomplish God's purposes. We certainly do not want to preempt a life because each life affects another. Each of you reading this e-mail is sharing in our real life journey, not just some contrived "reality show."

Because I was raised Catholic, I was trained from a young age to blindly obey and trust those in authority, so it is easy for me to trust the Word of God. Jesus tells us to have childlike faith in the Father. It is IMPOSSIBLE to please God without faith!

Tonight it is our fervent prayer that each of you grows in faith, trust and respect for the Creator of all things, both seen and unseen.

Now for some good news. Today Larry followed me around his bed with his eyes and blinked when asked to do so. He also held onto my two fingers tight enough to enable me to lift his arm off of the bed several times. AND..... tomorrow he will be transferred from Leigh Memorial to Portsmouth Naval Hospital.

Again if anything that I have shared in this e-mail has offended you, that is not my intent. If however you wish to be removed from this list, I will promptly comply.

Joyfully His,
Larry & Stacie

November 5, 2007
Subject: Continuing to Improve

Hi Everyone,

Well the medical transport people showed up at 3:30 this afternoon to take Larry over to the Portsmouth Naval Hospital and he was finally all settled in by about 6:00 pm.

Larry seemed much sharper tonight than he was at the other hospital, and he even squeezed my hand twice and followed me with his eyes as I walked around his bed.

Larry is in Room Five of the ICU. You can visit 24/7, but I ask you to please call me before you visit so that we don't have too many people there at the same time.

No flowers, fruits, vegetables or children are allowed in ICU, but cards and balloons are okay.

Thank you for all of your love, support and encouragement.

Joyfully His,
Larry & Stacie

November 6, 2007
Subject: Great News

Hi Everyone,

Let me say that the doctors at Portsmouth Naval Hospital rock! First of all because they are not compelled in any way to make decisions that would affect the profits of the stock holders, and second, because they are a teaching hospital, their thought processes and compassion are completely awesome.

Everyone loves Larry, and he has endeared himself to a large number of staff at the hospital over the last 14 months. I dare say that over half of the staff has been by to see him already and at least a quarter of those are born again believers. I cannot tell you how refreshing and encouraging it is to have friends on staff that will openly quote scripture and stand in agreement for Larry's complete restoration. The other hospital was so dark, lost and scary. As a matter of fact the reason that I had Larry transferred was because his doctor wanted to remove all sustenance and heavily medicate him so he would die.

Larry's vitals continue to strengthen, so they let him breath by himself today for more than an hour, then put the ventilator to the spontaneous mode, which functions exactly like his CPAP machine at home for sleep apnea. The plan is to remove the chest tube early tomorrow morning!

Okay are you sitting down? Larry opened his eyes and focused so sharply that he was able to move his eyes left and right 31 times as he followed my movements. Then he went back to sleep, but in his altered state of consciousness he hears everything that we are saying.

"Impossible ... is one of God's favorite words." -Max Lucado

Nothing is impossible with God. (Luke 1:37)

I am grateful for all of the witnesses to Larry's very humble condition, because they will only be able to give credit and glory to God for his restoration. There will be no doubt in anyone's mind that Larry's healing is by God's hand alone!

Joyfully His,
Larry & Stacie

November 7, 2007
Subject: Continued Improvement

Hi Everyone,

All is well. Larry is breathing great on his own and we were able to get some of his teeth back in his mouth.

He will be moved out of ICU to the oncology ward tomorrow or the next day.

Every valley shall be filled and every mountain and hill brought low; the crooked places shall be made straight and the rough ways smooth; and all flesh shall see the salvation of God. (Luke 3: 5-6)

This just means that God is in control and He is just, so He will make sure everything works out right.

Please continue to pray for Larry's complete restoration.

Joyfully His,
Larry & Stacie

November 8, 2007
Subject: Like Riding a Roller Coaster

Hello Everyone,

I have never liked roller coaster rides and this one is no different! When they took Larry off of the ventilator (yesterday), they moved his feeding tube to his right nostril. Last night when they checked the feeding tube, the contents were black indicating that his stomach was bleeding. At midnight they called to request permission to give him blood, and they ended up giving him three pints of blood and two pints of platelets.

Larry gave blood every 62 days religiously for years. I am reminded of a movie called "Pay It Forward." In this case, the forward seems to have come full circle.

Larry was pretty sleepy today but still managed to look at me for a while and grip my hand in his right hand tight enough so I could lift his arm like he was on the monkey bars.

I was feeling a bit discouraged when a preacher from Texas called us. I put him on speaker phone so Larry could hear him powerfully pray in faith and expectation for a miracle. (We do in fact need a miracle, and my God is big enough.) After he finished praying, he reminded me that if Larry only had half his brain that it would be more than enough since we only use about 10% of our brain anyway. It is not a big job for God to reroute Larry's neuropathways to utilize the undamaged portions.

If all goes well, Larry will be moving from ICU to the ward "where everybody knows his name," tomorrow.

Joyfully His,
Larry & Stacie

November 10, 2007
Subject: Out of ICU

Hello Everybody,

It was very late last night before Larry got all settled in from being transferred out of ICU, but everything is good. They discontinued all of his IV's and moved his feeding tube to his nose and are giving him all of his medications through his feeding tube. His vital signs remain solid, and he looks better every day. I continue to thank God for the renewal of his neuropathways.

"Nothing is impossible with God." (Luke 1:37)

Joyfully His,
Larry & Stacie

November 14, 2007
Subject: The Fight Goes On

Hello Everyone,

It is true that I have not written in a few days, and I did not mean to worry anyone. We have had some small challenges, but they are being compensated for on a daily basis and Larry continues to receive the best of care.

Tomorrow the endocrinologist is going to put a little tube down Larry's throat to look at the terrain. Then either

Friday or next week they are going to install a feeding port directly into his stomach so he can be fed three times a day without the risk of aspiration, which is possible when being fed through the tube down his nose. All of this is in preparation for bringing Larry home (rather than a nursing home). My son, Matthew, and his wife, Elaine, have agreed to move in with us to help with Larry's care. We are going to put on an addition, much like a mother-in-law apartment, so that they will have their privacy as well.

Without a battle there can be no victory! And both the battle and the victory belong to the Lord! With God all things are possible.

Joyfully His,
Larry & Stacie

November 15, 2007
Subject: Getting Better

Hello Everyone,

What a fascinating day we have had. First of all the senior doctor in charge of all of the residents and interns said that we are not going to go poking around in Larry unless we absolutely have to, thank God! This means that Larry did not have a little tube with a camera shoved down his throat today.

Larry had his eyes open a lot today and actually tracked me eight times with his gaze.

We are looking at the possibility of Larry coming home early next week. I spent most of my day with discharge planners and home health care people. There is a lot of information to digest in formulating plans.

The contractor came by today to draw up a plan and give an estimate for the addition to the house. I came into some complications concerning a loan, because I do not have a durable power of attorney. If Larry were able to consent, then they would give us the bank. We just keep finding ways for God to have to intercede in our life. I am just sorry to be soaking up so much of His time and attention.

We are so grateful for each and every one of you, and we are proud to call you our friends. Actually, you have become family.

My God shall supply all your needs through Christ Jesus, His only begotten son. The Lord is my shepherd, I shall not want. Nothing is impossible with God. I am thankful for a limitless Creator who handles all of the situations that I present Him with. Our complete faith and trust is in Him only. He makes everything easy by marking each straight path, all we need to do is follow the arrows.

Joyfully His,
Larry & Stacie

November 18, 2007
Subject: Closer to Coming Home

Hey Everyone,

Larry is doing better every day. Tomorrow he will have a feeding port installed into his tummy so he will no longer require a feeding tube down his nose. Woohoo! If everything goes well he could be coming home Tuesday or Wednesday.

Matt and Elaine will not be moving in after all, but they are just about three miles away and are willing to help anytime.

Oh, I received the bill for Larry's seven day ICU stay. It was $65,000, but the amount due is zero. It reminded me how much more Jesus has insured us for against eternal fire—priceless.

We are so thankful for all of the encouragement and support from friends, family, church and hospitals.

Joyfully His,
Larry & Stacie

November 19, 2007
Subject: Ooops!

Hello Everyone,

Well, some of you may have noticed that last night's update was dated the 25th. Ooops! My days are surely running together.

Larry had a very nice endoscopy today and received a lovely tummy piercing with a cute little tube so he can have his meals delivered directly to his stomach three times a day. Yeah, no more tubes down his nose or throat! The endoscopy revealed that he has a small ulcer that was responsible for the bleeding last week, but that it is on the mend quite nicely now and all of his blood values are nearly normal. Also, his temperature has normalized and the pneumonia is receding rapidly. Oh, Larry had his eyes open longer and more frequently today than on any day I can remember so far. Also, it now looks like he will not be discharged until next week.

When Larry was diagnosed with leukemia I was shocked and I thought that Larry was the last person who deserved to have this happen to him. Then I realized that Jesus didn't do anything to DESERVE being crucified. I do not understand why God allows bad things to happen, but I do know that

God uses every hurt inflicted upon His children in a tapestry of His sovereign design that we will see and comprehend when we get to Heaven.

Nothing is impossible with God. (Luke 1:37)

"Impossible is one of God's favorite words." ~ Max Lucado

Joyfully His,
Larry & Stacie

November 20, 2007
Subject: More Progress

Hello Everyone,

Imagine my surprise when I got to the hospital today and Larry was making noise! We do not know the meaning but I think he is trying to sing (sounds like humming) with the music that I have had playing nonstop in his room. He also had his eyes open most of the day and moved his neck and head a few times!

If we can get everything together by then, Larry will be coming home on Monday. I will be spending 24 hours at the hospital this weekend to prove that I can handle him at home by myself before they cut him loose.

Faith-filled words draw things out of the spiritual realm, where they do exist... into the natural realm, where they do not exist yet. Please join your faith-filled words with mine in agreement for Larry's complete restoration.

Joyfully His,
Larry & Stacie

November 25, 2007
Subject: Happy Thanksgiving

Hi Everybody and Happy Thanksgiving,

We are so grateful for all of the blessings that God has showered upon us this year, but the most notable for me is that my husband is alive and getting better daily. I spent from 8 p.m. Friday until 8 p.m. Saturday at the hospital doing everything the staff would normally do as sort of a test to see if I could handle all of the duties and responsibilities of being a full time care giver for Larry. One of the interns suggested that if I had the opportunity to care for Larry under their supervision and see how much was involved that I might change my mind and put him in a nursing home. Larry requires total assistance for everything so I learned how to handle elimination, feeding, medications, shots and assorted treatments. The reality is that I have been Larry's primary care giver since September 2006 when he had bilateral knee replacement. So I was more than ready for this challenge.

It doesn't look like Larry will be coming home until maybe Wednesday since he spiked a temperature today and there are some other anomalies that need to be worked out before they release him. I am glad for this.

Larry and I had been planning his chemo completion party earlier on the day he collapsed, and since I thought he was going to be released tomorrow, I planned a party for the marvelous staff.

Our son, Chef Matthew, has created a unique lasagna especially for the occasion. Each member of the staff will also receive a personalized thank you card with a laminated pocket sized message inside. Below is a copy of the message.

Our precious 4-J Family,

Words are not adequate to express our gratefulness for what you have meant to us. We were completely needy and dependent upon you for care yet you never once made us feel small, temporary, insignificant or worthless. You were always here with compassion and a smile. You have been the wind beneath our wings allowing us to courageously walk the road set before us. We could not have done this without your love and encouragement.

What you have meant to our lives can best be summed up by saying; you showed us Jesus. Your actions ministered to us ten times stronger than any sermon.

We thank you for the priceless blessings that you have been during this season in our lives and we pray eternal blessings for each of you.

We will always love you,
Larry & Stacie Adams

November 26, 2007
Subject: Blessing

Hi Everyone,

God put it on our hearts some time back to be a blessing and encouragement to all of the medical people and that is why everybody loves Larry. One evening while Larry was still in ICU, one of the doctors called me in a conference room to talk. He explained to me that the reason why the staff loved Larry so much was that he treated them special and didn't take his diagnosis out on others, particularly the medical staff. The doctor admitted that it is easy to become jaded, and that Larry had been able to sensitize so many hearts with his kind respect for them and his absolute love for Jesus.

Church worship today was awesome! The songs focused on restoration and the infallibility of God's promises.

It would be a huge personal favor if someone could e-mail me every scripture they could find concerning restoration. I am involved in a course of reading the Bible in 90 days, which does not facilitate any time for extracurricular study.

Joyfully His,
Larry & Stacie

November 28, 2007
Subject: Homecoming

Hi Everyone,

Yes, Larry came home today, and he couldn't be happier.

We gladly welcome any and all visitors, but it might be better if you called first on my cell phone.

We are so grateful for your continued prayers and help.

Joyfully His,
Larry & Stacie

Chapter 2

❧

December 5, 2007
Subject: A Challenging Week

Hello Everybody,

It has been a week since Larry came home, and I must say that it has been one of the most challenging weeks of my life. It has also been one of the most inspiring and humbling weeks as well due to the encouragement and help we have received from family, friends and friends that have become family.

I have to pat myself on the back for becoming the queen of adaptability for learning the nuances of Medicare, Tricare, insurance, social services, hospice and care giving procedures. Although it has been a whirlwind, we are starting to settle into somewhat of a routine, if any of this can be considered routine or normal in anyway.

We are so grateful for all of the blessings that God has bestowed upon us. That may sound stupid considering our circumstances but at least we live in America, we have a roof over our heads, food to eat, a nice bed to sleep in, and good transportation. This puts us in the top seven percent as the wealthiest people in the world! Plus we have a growing relationship with Jesus that continues to become more intimate every day.

I am convinced that no one could endure the circumstances we are facing with any peace or sanity without Jesus. There are those who may question my sanity because of the pure joy that I exude, but the truth is that the Holy Spirit is my comforter and strength, and we couldn't pull any of this off without His strength.

Joyfully His,
Larry & Stacie

December 6, 2007
Subject: Follow Your Destiny

Hello Everyone,

I was just going through some papers and came upon a journal entry that Larry made while in a prayer service about three months ago.

"Think of the books and songs that will never be written - works that will remain only in the mind of a person too fearful or selfish or lazy to dig for the treasure. I am convinced - that every choice one makes and every action one takes, or doesn't take, significantly affects the lives of everyone else. We are all connected to each other through our actions. Our decisions to act or not to act, to help or not to help - well, those choices create a ripple effect that can last for centuries."

When he originally showed this to me, he could not be sure if part of this had come from a book he had read. Regardless, he decided to own this philosophy and adhere to it for his life.

Each one of you has been uniquely hard wired to accomplish a specific destiny, but you get to choose whether or not you yield to fulfilling God's design for your life. Perhaps asking God what you can do for Him instead of asking Him what He can do for you will help each of us in seeing the plan God has for our lives.

Joyfully His,
Larry & Stacie

December 9, 2007
Subject: Dealing with Loneliness

Hello Everyone,

Today Larry is very animated, alert and responsive. Everyday gets a little better. A couple of days ago I believe Larry gave me three yes answers by blinking his eyes once, but we have not been able to reproduce it since.

A few times this week I have felt very lonely and am grateful that I can just zip into the bedroom and hug and kiss Larry to my heart's content. Still there is quite a void or emptiness as a result of the lack of response, so it is a bitter-sweet moment.

It's during these times that the Lord has shown me great insight into my relationship with Him. It takes two to have a relationship and two to have a conversation. Prayer is suppose to be a dialog not a monolog. So if I don't stop, wait and listen to what the Creator of all things (both seen and unseen) has to say to me, then He feels much the same loneliness that I feel with Larry right now.

Lord please forgive me for my laundry list of requests, as if You were Santa Clause to fulfill all my wants. Although I know that it is Your desire to bless Your children, I don't want to just use You. Help me to listen to Your voice so that we can have two-way communication. Jesus promised us in the New Testament that we can have a relationship with You. Please Lord, only You can fill this empty, lonely place in my heart.

It is our fervent hope that each of you will be blessed by the sharing of our most intimate thoughts and prayers with you as you have so graciously agreed to join us on our journey toward Heaven.

Joyfully His,
Larry & Stacie

December 17, 2007
Subject: Back to the hospital

Hi Everybody,

Yesterday evening Larry spiked a temperature that refused to be placated even by two heavy doses of Tylenol so at about 1:00 am I called a private medical transport to take him to Portsmouth Naval Hospital. Even though Larry is on the fast track for admissions it still took until 8 am to get him in a room and settled so I could come home and get a little rest before returning this afternoon. I have had three hours of sleep in the last 56.

All Your words are true; all Your righteous laws are eternal. (Psalm 119:160) Just like the laws of physics are true and unchangeable in this physical realm of existence; God's word, laws, and spirit are eternal - forever true, right, and just even though we cannot physically see them.

All we need to do is trust God, take Him at His word, and mix it with our faith. It is as easy as KISS (keep it simple silly). *Except we come to Him with child-like faith we cannot enter the kingdom of God. Everything that does not come from faith is sin.* (Romans 14:23) *May the God of hope fill you with all joy and peace as you trust in Him, so that you may overflow with hope by the power of the Holy Spirit.* (Romans 15:13) *I am confident of this; I will see the goodness of the Lord in the land of the living. Wait for the Lord; be strong and take heart and wait for the Lord.* (Psalm 27:13-14)

I was so encouraged today by Larry's attempt to form words in the purposeful movement of his lips while staring directly into my eyes. We are heavily engaged in spiritual warfare but the victory is already bought and paid for in the blood of Jesus. It doesn't rely on our strength but only our willingness to be used by God even during the most adverse circumstances without venting our own frustrations or feelings into the situation. We can only continue to do this with the most powerful weapon: the prayers that you offer in our behalf. Thank you.

Joyfully His,
Larry & Stacie

December 19, 2007
Subject:

Hello Everyone,

Larry spiked another temperature today, plus he also needed a pint of blood so he will not be coming home tomorrow like we thought. There is no clear cut explanation for what is causing the spikes or the low hemoglobin in medical terms, but in the spirit realm I can easily explain this phenomenon.

When Larry was diagnosed with leukemia, God gave him this scripture: *I will exalt You, O Lord, for You lifted me out of the depths and did not let my enemies gloat over me. O Lord my God, I called to You for help.* (Psalm 30:1)

Larry imitated God with His own words by speaking the end from the beginning in faith. For it is impossible to please

God without faith, and God's word does not return to Him in a void.

The Lord gave me this verse so that I too could visualize life after the storm: *You turned my wailing into dancing; You removed my sackcloth and clothed me in joy, that my heart may sing to You and not be silent. O Lord my God, I give You thanks forever.* (Psalm 30: 11-12)

Joy, not worry, is a fruit of the Spirit and a very powerful weapon. I know that people are often perplexed at my behavior under such perilous circumstances, but I choose to behave as a believer and not a doubter in God's love and faithfulness.

We love you guys and are grateful for your friendship and faith-filled prayers.

Joyfully His,
Larry & Stacie

December 20, 2007
Subject: Nothing is Impossible!

Hello Everyone,

It has become quite popular to condemn the "culture of death" that terrorists espouse without looking in our own backyard. I am speaking of the VERY common practice of deliberately neglecting helpless human beings by denying them food and water and thus cruelly starving them to death while calling it merciful! Even animals are not forced to suffer criminal neglect in being euthanized!

There are literally tens of thousands of Terri Schivo's on this planet that have been "euthanized," because they were simply deemed too inconvenient or costly to care for. The truth is that in our selfish society we do not want to be bothered with people who are helpless due to their age (infant or old) or diminished physical or mental capacity. Jesus himself said that in the last days the love of many will grow cold. If God wanted Larry dead, no amount of medical science could keep him alive!

A conversation took place only days after Larry's cardiac arrest on October 29th where his civilian doctor severely insisted that I allow him to withdraw all subsistence and medications from Larry until he died. He said this process would take about seven days! The doctor was emphatic that I allow him to murder Larry, because in his estimation he would be nothing but a vegetable the rest of his life and a terrible burden on me and maybe society. Remember, in this world, it is all about money!

Well surprise, surprise, surprise! The absolutely impossible happened today! Larry said his first word, and I have three witnesses outside of myself to verify it! What was the word Larry spoke you ask ... it was "when?"

Faith-filled words draw things out of the spiritual realm where they do exist ... into the physical realm where they do not exist yet. Fight the good fight of faith ... FIGHT FOR LIFE!

Joyfully His,
Larry & Stacie

December 25, 2007
Subject: Home for Christmas

Hello Everyone,

I know that I am late in sending this e-mail, but Larry came home from the hospital on Friday and has been very chipper and boisterous. Many times you can certainly discern that he is trying to communicate by the speech patterns he employs. At other times it sounds as if he is just singing to hear his own voice again.

Christmas is not necessarily a time or a place for us as much as it is a state of being. It's a feeling of being in the present without concern for the past or future. It is a chance to bask in the love of family, friends and the hope of an eternal life in the presence of the Eternal Being. Christmas is a day to remember the hope and love that God harbors in His heart for all of mankind by giving us His only begotten Son.

Although the circumstances of our life would appear to be a category five hurricane; we are totally assured of our eternal safety. This is my best Christmas ever, but it is certainly not my favorite.

May the God of hope fill you with joy and peace as you trust in Him, so that you may overflow with hope by the power of the Holy Spirit. (Romans 15:13)

Joyfully His,
Larry & Stacie

December 27, 2007
Subject: Good-bye Rocky

Hello Everybody,

Our little beagle went to doggie heaven today. He was nearly 16 years old, which would make him about 107 in dog years. Larry and I have always agreed that Rocky was the happiest dog either of us had ever known.

It's amazing to see the infinite plethora of resources that God uses to teach life lessons. Let me show you by using Rocky's life as a pet parable. Rocky was a recycled dog that we adopted from the SPCA. After we signed the papers, they told us that he was scheduled to be put to sleep the next day because he had been there so long. Rocky was so glad to have anyone pay him any attention that he would roll over and pee everywhere. As you can imagine the longer he stayed there the worse this condition became. I saw his potential, and Rocky did stop having the liquid response once he adopted Matthew as his very own boy. But Rocky never stopped being grateful for food, water, shelter and especially affection. He epitomized the ecstasy of being saved from imminent death.

So here is the moral of Rocky's life: Stay focused on what is truly important and give thanks and you will be happy. For us the focus is obeying the greatest commandment: *Love the Lord your God with all your heart, mind, soul and strength and love your neighbor as yourself.* (Matthew 22: 37-39)

We remind ourselves to give thanks in all circumstances, because we are so grateful for the love of God. We sincerely understand what the apostle Paul was talking about when he said: I give thanks in all circumstances (not FOR all) for I have learned what it is to be deprived and to abound. Although I hate what has happened to Larry, I am thankful to be able to trust God's love and eternal plans for us both. It makes me happy to be a blessing to God, and it fills me with joy unspeakable to think of how my behavior, under less than perfect circumstances, pleases Him.

Joyfully His,
Larry & Stacie

January 4, 2008
Subject: New Year's Challenge

Hello Everybody,

We hope that all of you had a great Christmas and a New Year's celebration filled with hope and love.

Larry was admitted to the hospital today for a severe urinary tract infection. I had been unable to control his temperature for the last two days. He should be home by next weekend.

All of my e-mail got sent into oblivion again but at least this time I know where it went; so if you wrote me something important in the last two weeks, please send it to me again.

We love all of you soooooooo much and appreciate everything that you do, particularly your prayers.

Joyfully His,
Larry & Stacie

January 9, 2008
Subject: Choose to Live

Hello Everyone,

Larry is back home again with a bunch of antibiotics but no temperature. He is feeling a whole lot better.

The story below really struck me that it could just as easily have Larry's name in it for all that he has been through, and I thought that you would enjoy the perspective.

\

ᴱ OF LIFE

Jerry was the kind of guy you love to hate. He was always in a good mood and always had something positive to say. When someone would ask him how he was doing, he would reply, "If I were any better, I would have to be twins!"

He was a unique manager because he had several waiters who had followed him around from restaurant to restaurant. The reason waiters followed Jerry was because of his attitude. He was a natural motivator. If an employee was having a bad day, Jerry was there telling them how to look on the positive side of the situation.

Seeing this style really made me curious, so one day I went up to Jerry and asked him, "I don't get it! You can't be a positive person all of the time. How do you do it?"

"Each morning I wake up and say to myself, 'Jerry, you have two choices today. You can choose to be in a good mood or you can choose to be in a bad mood.' I choose to be in a good mood. Each time something bad happens, I can choose to be a victim or I can choose to learn from it. I choose to learn from it," Jerry replied. "Every time someone comes to me complaining, I can choose to accept their complaining or I can point out the positive side of life. I choose the positive side of life."

"Yeah, right, it's not that easy," I protested.

"Yes it is," Jerry said. "Life is all about choices. When you cut away all the junk, every situation is a choice. You choose how you react to situations. You choose how people will affect your mood. You choose to be in a good mood or bad mood. The bottom line: It's your choice how you live life."

I reflected on what Jerry said. Soon thereafter, I left the restaurant industry to start my own business. We lost touch, but I often thought about him when I made a choice about life instead of reacting to it.

Several years later, I heard that Jerry did something you are never supposed to do in a restaurant business: He left the back door open one morning and was held up at gunpoint by three armed robbers. While trying to open the safe, his hand, shaking from nervousness, slipped off the combination. The robbers panicked and shot him. Luckily, Jerry was found relatively quickly and rushed to the local trauma center.

After 18 hours of surgery and weeks of intensive care, Jerry was released from the hospital with fragments of the bullets still in his body. I saw Jerry about six month after the incident. When I asked him how he was, he replied, "If I were any better, I'd be twins. Wanna see my scars?"

I declined to see his wounds, but did ask him what had gone through his mind as the robbery took place.

"The first thing that went through my mind was that I should have locked the back door," Jerry said. "Then, as I lay on the floor, I remembered that I had two choices: I could choose to live, or I could choose to die. I chose to live."

"Weren't you scared? Did you loose consciousness?" I asked.

"The paramedics were great," Jerry continued. "They kept telling me I was going to be fine. But when they wheeled me into the emergency room, I saw the expressions on the faces of the doctors and nurses and got really scared."

"In their eyes, I read, 'He's a dead man.' I knew I needed to take action."

"What did you do?" I asked.

"Well, there was a big burly nurse shouting questions at me," said Jerry. "She asked if I was allergic to anything. 'Yes,' I replied. The doctors and nurses stopped working as they waited for me to complete my reply and say what it was I was allergic to. I took a deep breath and yelled, 'Bullets!'

"Over their laughter, I told them, 'I am choosing to live. Operate on me as if I am alive, not dead.'" Jerry lived thanks to the skill of the doctors, but also because of his amazing attitude. I learned from him that every day we have the choice to live fully. ~Author Unknown

Joyfully His,
Larry & Stacie

January 10, 2008
Subject: Be Prepared

Hello Everyone,

All is well. I will be going to a business convention this weekend and Larry will be cared for by my brother and my son Matthew.

I have been reading; "The Holiest of All" by Andrew Murray (An Exposition of the Epistle to the Hebrews). The following statement truly summarizes the life of the believer: "God has given you such a High Priest that you might live an impossible life, a life above all sense and reason, a supernatural life in the power of His Son."

This would also explain why people think that Larry and I are weird or unreasonable about our faith in God. We are at complete peace about what God is doing in and through us.

Here is the big picture: Everybody wants to go to Heaven but nobody wants to die. Today I made arrangements for Larry and I to be buried together in the cemetery behind our church. We sincerely pray that each of you have considered and prepared for your final destination both physically and spiritually. If you haven't, we hope this e-mail prompts you to do so now.

Joyfully His,
Larry & Stacie

January 23, 2008
Subject: Still Doing the Impossible!

Hi Everyone,

Larry has been doing some absolutely impossible things and so from now on he should be referred to as Miracle Larry. Last week we finally got all the equipment necessary to lift Larry out of bed and into a special reclining rolling chair. His nurse showed me how to use it, and Larry responded by smiling and laughing especially when we got him out in the living room with the Christmas tree still twinkling. His nurse had to go back to the office for some more supplies, and while she was gone I was able to have my neighbor, Sandy, come over and see Larry laughing at her in the kitchen. Now she has a new vision and can stop having post-traumatic stress flash backs form the last time she saw him in the kitchen ... looking dead.

When Larry's nurse returned, she said the staff agrees that Larry has shown way too much progress to be eligible for hospice anymore and in fact he needs to go to a residential rehabilitation program! Now we are waiting for his doctor to call us back and tell us how to make this happen.

Lover boy Larry gave me between 30 and 50 kisses on Monday. He also has a repertoire of about ten words that are very clear, and his aide is his favorite person to talk to. He drinks water and juice from a dropper without any problems. From a medical stand point none of these things are even remotely possible with Larry's diagnosis. I have never disputed the accuracy of the diagnosis. So, recall how I have asked each of you to pray for the restoration of Larry's neuropathways and the renewal of his body? Well these manifestations are the direct result of God answering those prayers.

I have two CT Scans and two EEGs from two separate facilities that confirm that even breathing should be a tenuous possibility. Larry's progression is living proof that God not only exists, but that He has gladly intervened to demonstrate just how all powerful He is. In this case, the FACTS PROVE GOD. We are so thrilled and honored to be a part of what God is doing in the lives of all the medical staff that are awakening to a higher calling than just mere science.

On the home front, God has sent friends and workmen with prophetic words of encouragement and many signs and wonders in the form of personal testimonies of people who have recovered and been fully restored from much harsher situations than Larry's. The repetitive theme is that God has us covered. I submit to you that God has each of us covered, and we have absolutely nothing to fear or to worry about. This is impossible for the world to understand, but we are at complete peace knowing that the Creator of all things seen and unseen has us covered. We are stress free and grateful.

Joyfully His,
Larry & Stacie

January 27, 2008
Subject: Woooooooo - Hoooooooo

Hello Everybody,

Tuesday will make exactly three months since Larry had a cardiac arrest, although it seems longer ago than that to me.

Yesterday my brother and his family came over and we did some experiments with Larry. He drank Pepsi and ate apple sauce! This morning Larry asked me for more apple sauce, and he ate four ounces!

Larry makes progress every day, but it is still very challenging. Whenever I start to get discouraged or lose hope, I am always encouraged by scripture. Today's scripture is this:

I am still confident of this; I will see the goodness of the Lord in the land of the living. Wait for the Lord. Be strong, take heart and wait for the Lord. (Psalm 27:13). We love and appreciate all of you and certainly thank God continuously for your loving prayers.

Joyfully His,
Larry & Stacie

January 31, 2008
Subject: Larry's in ICU

Hello Everyone,

I just got home from the Naval Hospital.

Yes my sweetie-pie was just as happy as a little yellow ducky yesterday, but today he spiked a temperature that I could not control. He also had two very serious wall-to-wall bouts of diarrhea with no end in sight. As it turns out, Larry has a touch of pneumonia. His vitals are not pretty, he has a urinary tract infection and he is also suffering from an intestinal infection. The stark contrast between today and yesterday is so startling that it just smacks of spiritual warfare.

Just to bring you up to speed, Larry is going to a residential rehabilitation facility, but that will be delayed a bit as a result of this event. But it may also work to our advantage so that he may get a higher priority placement at our first choice facility.

A righteous man may have many troubles, but the Lord delivers him from them ALL. He protects all his bones, not one of them is broken. (Psalms 34:19).

No matter what the circumstances are, we are trusting the Lord our God totally.

Joyfully His,
Larry & Stacie

February 5, 2008
Subject: Thanksgiving Every Day

Hello Everyone,

Larry is doing better. Friday he received two units of blood, tons of antibiotics and was transferred out of ICU. He should be coming home or to a rehabilitation facility on Wednesday or Thursday.

A friend recently sent me the following excerpt and it blessed and focused me so well that I could not resist sharing it with each of you.

Dear God:

I want to thank You for what You have already done. I am not going to wait until I see results or receive rewards; I am thanking You right now. I am not going to wait until I feel better or things look better; I am thanking You right now. I am not going to wait until people say they are sorry or until they stop talking about me; I am thanking You right now. I am not going to wait until the pain in my body disappears; I am thanking You right now. I am not going to wait until my financial situation improves; I am going to thank You right now. I am not going to wait until the children are asleep and the house is quiet; I am going to thank You right now. I am not going to wait until I get promoted at work or until I get the job; I am going to thank You right now. I am not going to wait until I understand every experience in my life

*that has caused me pain or grief; I am thanking You right
now. I am not going to wait until the journey gets easier or
the challenges are removed; I am thanking You right now.
I am thanking You because I am alive. I am thanking You
because I have walked around the obstacles. I am thanking
You because I have the ability and the opportunity to do
more and do better. I'm thanking You because FATHER,
YOU haven't given up on me.*

God is just so good and He's good all the time. *In everything give thanks: for this is the will of God in Christ Jesus
concerning you.* (1Thess 5:18)
I cannot emphasize this enough; your prayers of faith
and agreement on our behalf are the most marvelous gift that
you could ever give us.

Joyfully His,
Larry & Stacie

February 8, 2008
Subject: Making a Move

Hello Everyone,

Tomorrow morning Larry is going to be transferred
from the Naval Hospital to a rehabilitation facility which is
located not even a quarter mile from Matt and Elaine.
Larry is eligible to receive up to 100 days of skilled
nursing care under our insurance plan. Because he still has
an infection, he will be receiving long term antibiotics. But
it also means that he will have a private room. Visiting hours
are flexible, and I encourage visitors. Right now the amount
of rehabilitation he will receive is minimal until he shows
more aptitude.

You know, our life may be complicated, but we are so at peace because we don't have any regrets. A wise woman once told me that when you are old and in the autumn of life it is not the things that you have done that will cause you to look back at your life with regret but the things that you failed to do. I hope the little pearls of wisdom below will help each of us keep our lives in perspective.

No Regrets:

"Life is too short for drama and petty things, so laugh hard, love truly and forgive quickly. Live while you are alive. Tell the people you love that you love them at every opportunity. Forgive now those who made you cry, you might not get a second chance. Lost time can never be found." ~ Author Unknown

Joyfully His,
Larry & Stacie

February 18, 2008
Subject: Rehabilitation

Hi Everyone,

Due to circumstances beyond our control, Larry was moved to his new digs last Tuesday instead of last Monday. It has been a very challenging week filled with adaptation and sometimes chaos.

Rehabilitation started cautiously last Thursday. Today marked his third day of training and he is progressing nicely. After kissing me good-bye he said, "I love you" so that all of the physical therapists heard him! We are so grateful to have this opportunity to do rehabilitation! I am so proud of Larry. His attitude is great, and he is trying so hard to do everything that they ask him to do even though it is such an incredible struggle.

During the past two weeks, I confess that I have allowed myself to grow weary as I have watched four Christian friends lose their battles to live. I took my eyes off of Jesus and looked at the storm. God has not called any of us to do anything or to experience anything that Jesus didn't already endure. It's impossible to please God without faith, and if we are not pleasing God, then what is the point in living at all? Can anyone truly be satisfied by living for themselves or even another human being? The moral of this experience is that our four friends died victoriously because they each died trusting in their almighty Creator.

I have yet another confession. (Maybe because it is Lent, I feel the need to purge my soul.) Some people have made comments about how dedicated and loyal I am to Larry as if I am some kind of saint for doing what I am doing. First of all Larry deserves far more love and loyally than I am capable of giving him, because of all the lives he has saved, including mine. Second, my previous marriage was a tragic disaster because I lacked these traits. Third, my life was radically transformed when I turned my pathetic existence over to my Lord Jesus to fix and to make it worth living. So if I am viewed as a saint, it is only by the grace of God and not the result of my own doing. It is because of the noble character of Jesus that lives in me and in every one of you that has chosen Jesus as your rescuer.

Joyfully His,
Larry & Stacie

February 19, 2008
Subject: Perspective

Hello Everyone,

I had the honor of attending a home-going celebration (funeral) for our former pastor today. God once again affirmed that He can use ANYONE and ANY CIRCUMSTANCES to His glory.

This pastor was a humble man who was grateful for every day that God gave him. This man was a perfect example of how God uses the simple and socially unacceptable to shame those who are self-righteous and proud in their own eyes. God used this man and his wife to plant more than 500 churches, as well as free medical clinics, orphanages, Bible Colleges, and schools around the world. All of this would be impressive enough, but now consider that this man spent 17 years of his life as a hardened criminal and a hopeless heroin addict! Only God can transform a life in such a remarkable way!

This is a prime example of how God does not call the equipped, He equips the called. This man's pathetic life wasn't worth zero because he lacked hope. But in desperation, he called out to God and surrendered himself totally to the hands of his merciful Creator. God in turn used him mightily.

Larry and I have always dreamed of being used by God in some marvelous way. So what has stopped us? In some ways our former pastor had an advantage, his life had nowhere to go but up. The lures of security, complacency and status (or fear of what people might think of us) are very seductive elements. America, like Babylon, has become a very dangerous place in terms of extravagant luxury and seeking our own comfort zone. There is no place more dangerous than friendly captivity. I have come to the conclusion that it is time for us to take our faith to the next level, which means stepping out of the boat. We have been radically saved by a radical Savoir, and we are ripping off the blindfold and gloves.

We boldly proclaim our belief, steadfast faith, trust and reliance on the promises of God, and we will not be deceived by the enemy into second guessing our God, in Jesus' name. Amen.

Joyfully His,
Larry & Stacie

February 25, 2008
Subject: Time Flies

Hello Everyone,

Well, Larry has been at the rehab facility now for almost two weeks, and the time has just zoomed by for me. He has had about seven days of evaluation and training now and does something new each day. Yesterday (Sunday) was a day off for him, but he was very chipper and you can see just how grateful he is by the number of kisses he gives. Last week he kissed both of his physical therapy technicians, and yesterday he kissed our sister-in-law and said "I love you."

I read this book last week that truly renewed my mind and spirit and encouraged me immensely. It is called: "Hung by the Tongue," by Francis Martin. It emphasized the fact that even God created the universe with the words of His tongue and how important our words are. In fact we will be judged by every word that proceeds out of our mouths. This book is a great little refresher course and an easy read.

One of my favorite verses in life is: *Whatever is true, noble, right, pure, lovely, or admirable - if anything is excel-*

lent or praiseworthy- think about such things. (Phil 4:8). It is impossible to be depressed, if I stay focused on these things.

A friend of ours now stationed in Cuba sent this to us and I hope it helps you keep your life's purpose in perspective as it has for us.

Our True Identity...

Our deepest fear is not that we are inadequate. Our deepest fear is that we are powerful beyond measure. It is our light, not our darkness that most frightens us. We ask ourselves, who am I to be brilliant, gorgeous, talented, or fabulous? Actually who are you not to be? You are a child of God. You playing small does not serve the world. There's nothing enlightened about shrinking, so that other people won't feel insecure around you. We are all meant to shine, as children do. We are born to make manifest the glory of God that is within us. It's not just in some of us; it's in everyone. And as we let our own light shine, we unconsciously give other people permission to do the same. As we're liberated from our own fear, our presence automatically liberates others." - Marianne Williamson (A Return to Love: Reflections on the Principles of "A Course in Miracles," Harper Collins, 1992. Chap 7 Sec 3)

Joyfully His,
Larry & Stacie

March 3, 2008
Subject: Pictures Wanted

Hello Everyone,

Larry is doing very well today and has the twinkle back in his eyes. He has been working at overcoming another bout of pneumonia all week, and the nebulizer treatments have helped a great deal. Please! I cannot stress this enough! Please send us a picture of your family for our prayer board in Larry's room. He has started actively praying with me over each of your faces, and he is able to recognize more people each day! He has actually begun to answer questions with head nods for yes and no responses. Prayer in the spirit does not require our lips or our minds, so let Larry do this for you.

I saw a DVD called: "A Vow to Cherish," about a man whose wife developed Alzheimer's disease and how he dealt with her, their kids and his job. At one point someone suggested that because she no longer knew who he was that she would do just as well in a nursing home. He replied that even if she didn't know who he was; that he would never forget who she was.

I know who Larry is whether he knows me or not, and more importantly I know to Whom he belongs. Larry and Jesus loved me even when I was mean and cranky and self-focused. They have been nothing but patient with me no matter how ugly my behavior has been (thank God for less frequent episodes) and have not given up on me. It is inconceivable that I should give up on him now when he is the most vulnerable and helpless!

A business mentor of ours gave me a book called: "If Satan Can't Steal Your Joy....." by Jerry Savell. Joy is a supernatural fruit of the spirit as well as an amazing weapon for overcoming evil in every form as it tries to come against you. I regularly confess that the joy of the Lord is my strength, but this book has explained how and why joy works against evil.

I am going to send each of you an e-mail entitled "Humbling," that shows just how small earth is in comparison to the infinite, ever expanding universe our God has created. It is very interesting to see where we fit into the big picture.

Joyfully His,
Larry & Stacie

March 5, 2008
Subject: Larry Keeps Getting Better

Hello Everybody,

Well we sure have a lot to report! Larry's swallow test went much better than expected, so his speech therapist is aggressively introducing a number of thickened liquids as well as ice cream and pudding. Her goal is to get him back to eating solid foods so that we can remove the feeding tube!

This last weekend Larry's physical therapist drove over to the Eastern Shore of Virginia on her own time, using her vehicle to get what I call a Frankenstein Table. The purpose is to help Larry stand upright, which will strengthen his bones and lessen the chances for developing bed sores. Her goal is to get Larry strong enough to assist in transfers from bed to a chair or even from a chair to the van.

Yesterday was the official care plan meeting, and they made a few changes to his diet and vitamin regimen based upon the fact that he has lost 18 pounds in the last 21 days. Our plan is for Larry to come home on May 21st and hopefully receive continued physical and occupational therapy.

Now for a serious praise report! Six months ago I had a mammogram that disclosed something troubling. Today during the follow up mammogram, it is totally gone! My God is so very good to me!

This is how good God is; I was socially retarded as a child, but God has taught me how to be a girlfriend and has blessed me with some of the best girlfriends on the planet. I am certain that loving relationships are why God created us and the thing that He enjoys the most.

Joyfully His,
Larry & Stacie

March 11, 2008
Subject: A Monumental Day

Hi Everyone,

Yesterday was a monumental day of firsts! Larry sucked thickened liquid through a straw, went up to 30 degrees on his Frankenstein Table for nearly an hour, made the permanent transition from a Geri Chair to a high back wheel chair and, last but certainly not least, he ate vanilla ice cream! Oh, and today his physical therapist will be taking his Frankenstein Table to 40 degrees.

On the neurological front, Larry is regularly responding with "yes" and "no" answers accompanied by head nods or shakes, as well as initiating meaningful hand movements. Yesterday he reached up and grabbed my hand and then slowly pulled me to him. Then later he reached out quite far for his shoes as if he was just going to put them on for himself. I am sure that he soon will.

A friend of ours, out of her deep love for Larry, brought up an interesting question. Why Larry? Of all the people in the world who probably deserve bad things to happen to them, why has all of this happened to someone so nice and especially to such a faithful man of God? Why has God allowed this to happen to Larry of all people?

God causes His sun to rise on the evil and the good, and sends rain on the righteous and the unrighteous. (Psalms 37:19)

God has given permission to include some "Why Larry" segments to this and future e-mail updates.

When Larry was diagnosed with leukemia we went through a process that revolutionized our lives. But what stood out in our thoughts the most was how was it possible for any person to face such an ordeal without God? That thought suddenly propelled Larry to share Jesus with everyone who came near him. How many times can you remember us asking in astonishment, how do people endure these types of ordeals without God? More horrifying than ANY diagnosis was the prospect that some person could spend eternity in Hell, because we were too selfish or lazy to act on what we know is the right thing to do.

So, why Larry? Why not Larry? Larry is Heaven bound regardless of the timing. Who better? Certainly his trust and faithful testimony bless and please God very much, just as our friend Dixie Smith's courage and enthusiasm did. Dixie finally succumbed to cancer but her beautiful testimony is an inspiration to us all. Truly the world needs afflicted believers that stand as shining examples of hope and faith to a suffering and dying world.

Joyfully His,
Larry & Stacie

March 22, 2008
Subject: More about "Why Larry?"

Hello Everyone,

Larry is looking well despite the fact that he has aspiration pneumonia in both lungs and some serious compression injuries (bed sores) on his back side. His speech therapist is the only person authorized to feed him by mouth, and as soon as this pneumonia is cleared up, she will start feeding him with electrodes attached to his throat to stimulate more swallowing. This just conjures up comical pictures when you combine the imagery of the electrodes on his neck with the Frankenstein Table therapy! It sounds like the makings for a Rocky Horror Theme Park to me!

Why Larry commentary:

If your faith is never tested how do you know if you have faith at all? We all believe things but faith is more than belief. Faith is standing firmly in the face of some adversity (big or small) and trusting God to be God on your behalf.

The adventures of Paul the apostle are a prime example of how we can expect our faith to be tested by God's enemy and how to be an overachiever in spiritual warfare.

Our prayer for each of you this week is that you put on the full armor of God, so that when the day of evil comes, you may be able to stand your ground. And after you have done everything you know to do, that you would continue to stand in faith knowing that your Heavenly Father loves you and wants only good for you. May you always remember: The harder the struggle; the greater the reward.

Joyful Resurrection Day,
Larry & Stacie

March 26, 2008
Subject: Amazing

Hello Everyone,

Yesterday Larry was elevated to a 55-degree angle on the Frankenstein Table! He is looking really good, so after therapy I was able to take him out in the sunshine for about 15 minutes until I thought he might be getting sunburned.

Remember me telling you that Larry would be coming home in May because that is when the insurance runs out for his rehabilitation as an inpatient? Well, I have been talking to God about the need for a van to transport Larry once he comes home and that it probably needed to have a lift as well. A flier came in the mail on Monday from a dealership stating that they still had brand new 2007 vans to get rid of. I went online to check out the Kelly Blue Book on it and spent some time talking with God. He told me to offer them a particular amount and then just walk away. When I got to the dealership and saw the van, I was nearly too embarrassed to make the offer because it was $6,000 less than the sticker price. But wouldn't you know they accepted it!

Now here is the kicker, we ended up paying $2,000 less for the 2007 van, brand new with a lifetime power train warranty than we did for a three-year-old used van (same kind) with 60,000 miles on it back in 2000. Isn't that amazing? But that is not the end of the Godincidence... Chrysler will pay up to $1,000 in assistance for a chair lift to be installed!

I know that my God meets all my needs according to His riches in glory by Christ Jesus, but I certainly didn't expect this prayer that our Sunday school class prayed to come to fruition in just three days. I guess I had fallen into the habit of thinking that in order to get anything from God I would have to pray long enough or be good enough, or earn it. Make no mistake, this van is a gift from God and we are very grateful for this tool.

Why Larry Commentary:

Each of us is hardwired for a specific destiny and purpose in the body of Christ. When we have accomplished our quest and finished our journey here, we are called home to be with our Father. Our prayer for each of you is that you will make the most of each moment you are given so that you may find your purpose, be satisfied, and fulfill your destiny.

Joyfully His,
Larry & Stacie

March 27, 2008
Subject: Response

Hello Everyone,

I received an e-mail in response to yesterdays' update that I wanted to share with you. This lady is a cherished friend of ours and a fervent Bible student.

"Awesome story about how you got the van & chair lift! Thank you for sharing. I never knew anyone personally that could actually hear from God like that. I've only heard preachers talking about it. I'm sooooooooo jealous, Stacie! (Not of the van, but that you can hear such clear instructions from God.) I wonder if that makes you a prophet? Question! When you talk to God are you speaking to and addressing

God the Father, Jesus, or the Holy Ghost? Maybe I am talking to the wrong one!"

My dear Friend,

I am grateful and honored that you would like to have a more intimate relationship with God, because you admire the relationship that I share with Him. That is exactly what the world should be yearning for as a result of our faith in action. There are so many types of prayers and reasons for praying that there certainly cannot be one specific formula (so to speak) in order to accomplish the desired outcome, it is important to know why you are praying and what you expect as the outcome of your effort. Most of the time I just talk to God like I would speak to my husband, and have conversations with Him about ALL SORTS of things whether it is about my feelings or science or social events. Sometimes I just concentrate on how immense and awesome God is or how wonderful our High Priest is, or how holy and good His Spirit is. In whatever person of the Trinity best suits the situation and helps you to fellowship in your mind's eye, then that is the image of God that you should look upon in order to fulfill your need at the moment. God knows your heart, your motives and your intent, and He loves just spending time with you. Just love on God with a pure heart and you will be blessed by His response. God does not play favorites, He loves us all. But He certainly enjoys hanging out with the children that are loving and obedient better than He does those who are stubborn and rebellious. God speaks to all of His children, so it takes practice to listen and trust to believe that it is His voice we are hearing and not our own. But practice makes perfect. I hope this answer has helped you, but clearly it is only the tip of the iceberg. I would like to write more on the subject of developing a great relationship with God. Would it be alright with you if I used your e-mail (minus your name of course) as part of a series of e-mails on this subject?

We love all of you so much,
Larry & Stacie

April 2, 2008
Subject: The Next Generation

Hello Everyone,

Larry continues to progress every day. Last week his physical therapist took him up to 65 degrees on the Frankenstein Table, and he is clearly responding with "yes" and "no" answers to her questions. His occupational therapist has returned after a three-week absence so he can get back to work on his hand movements. Overall Larry is looking very healthy.

Last Friday, 11 middle school students from our church came over and blessed us by painting our garage, laying and leveling a bunch of bricks and raking our yard of all the debris from over the winter. What a tremendous thrill it is to see kids helping others and being proud to speak about Jesus. It is just so refreshing to see the next generation putting action behind their faith.

Why Larry Commentary:

I just love how the Apostle Paul provides us scripture that we can pray in the first person and confer upon ourselves as he does in Galatians 2:20: *I have been crucified in Christ, it is no longer I who lives but Christ Jesus lives in me and the life that I now live in the flesh I live by faith in the Son of God, who loved me, and gave himself for me.*

Nothing in this world can harm Larry; he has been sanctified by the sacrificial life and blood of Jesus. He is truly living his life on God's time now in the realm of the Holy Spirit. He can turn neither to the left nor to the right but only walk the narrow path designed for him, just as Jesus walked the narrow corridor to His sacrificial gift of love for Larry and each of us.

How easy would it be if we didn't have to make any decisions; if God always told us exactly what to do and all we had to do was obey? Well, that pretty much summarizes where Larry is at right now. But we don't have to be incapacitated to hear from or obey God. What distinguishes Christianity from all of the other religions on earth is our ability to have an intimate personal relationship with our Creator, and it is impossible to have a relationship without two-way communication!

Our prayer for each of you is that you enter into the Holiest of Holies, behind the veil that Jesus' blood ripped apart to fulfill God's dream of being reunited to His children in a loving relationship.

Joyfully His,
Larry & Stacie

April 3, 2008
Subject: Totally Vertical - Dude

Hi Everyone,

I hope you are sitting down, because Larry stood up totally vertical for 11 minutes yesterday keeping his legs straight and supporting his own weight in a standing box. Yes, it has been six months since he last stood upright. Not only was he able to effectively communicate with his physical therapist using affirmative or negative gestures, but he also communicated that his knee was hurting so they gave him some Tylenol. Then he purposefully tried to remove one of his hand splints for the occupational therapist and fully lifted his arm in order to reach for Matt's shirt while laughing and being precocious. This is certainly a quantum leap in performance. And of course none of these remarkable improvements are consistent with his diagnosis and can only be attributed to the miraculously working hand of God.

Joyfully His,
Larry & Stacie

April 11, 2008
Subject: Jack him up!

Hello Everybody,

Today Larry went to 90 degrees on the Frankenstein table for five minutes! Now we just need to build the time that he is able to tolerate it. Also, we went to the hospital for a Barium Swallow test now that his pneumonia is cleared up, and he is able to swallow thickened food very well, but not liquids. The speech therapist is going to attach electrodes to his throat to see if that will stimulate a better swallowing response. (More pictures of Frankenstein dance in my head)

For those of you who may have missed this story the other day, I am repeating it and following through with another response to her question about prayer. The following words in brackets are those of a dear and faithful friend of ours and are used with her permission:

[Awesome story about how you got the van & chair lift! Thank you for sharing. I never knew anyone personally that could actually hear from God like that. I've only heard preachers talking about it. I'm sooooooooo jealous, Stacie! (Not of the van, but that you can hear such clear instructions from God.) I wonder if that makes you a prophet?

Question! When you talk to God are you speaking to and addressing God the Father, Jesus, or the Holy Ghost? Maybe I am talking to the wrong one!]

I cannot begin to explain how unexpected it is for someone who used to be so proud of being called the "Dragon Lady" to be thought of in such a good way.

The day that I completely surrendered my life to the will of God and promised Him that I would live my life to copy Jesus' wasn't a commitment to any religion or any denomination of Christianity. The lure for me to submit my will to imitate Jesus was for the purpose of having a relationship; not rules, laws or regulations imposed upon me by any person. Outside of Satan worshipers, Christians are the only group of people who have two-way communication with their deity.

Just as you would talk to your best friend about even insignificant things, I speak to God like that in my thoughts all day long. I am getting better about asking Him what He thinks before I open my mouth, and periodically I remind God that I have given Him permission to put a guard over my mouth. My God is too big for my finite brain to comprehend and I fear putting Him in a box in my mind. He knows my heart better than I do. When I confess a sin, that is not when He finds out about it. Whether I am interceding, praising, giving thanks, or in supplication, I can only have that relationship by and through the blood of Jesus that allows me, and all of mankind, entrance to the throne room of God.

Remember that prayer does not change God, but it will change the heart of the person doing the praying.

Ephesians chapter four is the perfect place to read about the power of unity. In verse six it explains how God is One, and in verse 11 how spiritual gifts are given for the unifying of the Body of Christ.

Our prayer for each of you this week is that you be imitators of God as dear children. To walk unified (yes, unified) in love, as Christ also has loved us and gave Himself for us, as an offering and a sacrifice that is well pleasing to God.

Joyfully His,
Larry & Stacie

April 20, 2008
Subject: Voice Recognition

Hi Everybody,

This week has been very eventful and mostly fun filled. Larry is standing for longer durations and building his stamina and eating a little more each time. But the really big news is that just after Larry's last chemo session (and just days before his heart stopped) he made a mini-cassette recording of some positive affirmations and read scripture in anticipation for his fourth and final chemo hospitalization. I had a reason to dig out the cassette recorder last week and was very pleasantly shocked to have Larry's sweet words on tape. I wish each of you could have witnessed the look on Larry's face when I played his voice for him saying the most awesome things! This spiritual shot in the arm could not have come at a better time.

Speaking of timing, I came home last Thursday to find a custom-made ramp fully installed at our front door! I cannot explain how humbled and thankful we are to have a church family to look after us like this.

Don't tell God how Big your storm is; tell the storm how Big your God is!

Joyfully His,
Larry & Stacie
April 29, 2008
Subject: Six Months Ago

Hi Everyone,

Yes, six months ago today, Larry died in our kitchen for about 23 minutes. His color was purple-black and the noise he made was that of a death rattle. I knew enough to know that I needed to call for help before I started CPR, so I simultaneously called 911 and ran across the street to tell my neighbor to come as quick as she could.

The rescue team entered to relieve me at CPR, and I heard the supervisor softly say to one of the EMTs "Do you see the color?" Then he slowly shook his head from side to side. I was an EMT briefly in the late 70s, so I knew what he was actually saying to the medics was, "He's a goner, but go through the motions anyway." As I was properly relieved at doing CPR, I started praying and calling on the name of Jesus repeatedly with my neighbor in agreement. We stood fervently on the promises and faithfulness of God for Larry. Because Larry, my neighbor and myself have a passionate personal relationship with Jesus, we knew we could expect Him to bring Larry back at our request.

In the meantime, the rescue supervisor interpreted my prayers as the ramblings of a hysterical woman and three times he broached me to reassure me that they were doing everything that they could. Little did he know that I already knew that nothing they could do would have made any difference. Thinking that I was going insane and trying to placate me, he ordered the EMTs to shock Larry a third time (which is strictly not protocol) but, what the heck, he was already dead anyway, so what could it hurt? The two EMTs flinched backward when Larry's heart instantly resumed beating!

Larry was resurrected because God intervened to override the normal course of nature. God is faithful to honor ALL His promises to those who BELIEVE.

"Again I say to you that if two of you agree on earth concerning anything that they ask, it will be done for them by My Father in heaven. For where two or three are gathered together in My name, I am there in the midst of them." ~Jesus (Matthew 18:19-20)

"And whatever things you ask in prayer, BELIEVING, you will receive." ~Jesus (Matthew 21:22)

"So I say to you, ask, and it will be given you; seek and you will find, knock, and it will be opened to you. For everyone who asks receives, and he who seeks finds, and to him who knocks it will be opened." ~Jesus (Luke 11:9-10)

"And whatever you ask in My name, that I will do, that the Father may be glorified in the Son. If you ask anything in My name, I WILL DO IT FOR YOU." ~Jesus (John 14:13-14)

"If you abide in Me, and My words abide in you, you will ask what you desire, and it shall be done for you. By this My Father is glorified, that you bear much fruit; so you will be My disciples." ~Jesus (John 15:7-8)

"You did no choose Me, but I chose you and appointed you that you should go and bear fruit, and that your fruit should remain, that whatever you ask the Father in My name He may give you." ~Jesus (John 15:16)

"And in that day you will ask Me nothing. Most assuredly, I say to you, whatever you ask the Father in My name He will give you. Until now you have asked nothing in My name.

Ask, and you will receive, that your joy may be full." ~Jesus (John 16:23-24)

"In that day you will ask in My name, and I do not say to you that I shall pray the Father for you; for the Father Himself loves you, because you have loved Me, and have BELIEVED that I came forth from God." ~Jesus (John 16:26-27)

Please note that the words in all caps are my emphasis, but that all of the quotes are from Jesus' lips, not any human interpretation. Call us gullible, but we believe every word that proceeds from the mouth of God.

Larry and I are BELIEVERS, not Baptist or Catholic or Pentecostal. Larry and I go to church because it is good to associate with people who are like-minded, and we all benefit from those friendships. But going to church does not make you a Christian any more than being a Christian makes you a believer. Believing requires faith, and faith comes from hearing the word of God. If faith came through problematic experiences, we would ALL be faith giants by now!

Are you longing for a resurrection in your soul (the culmination of your mind, will and emotions) and a revival of God's presence in your life? Are you tired of just hearing about the glorious manifestations of His power in the past or in someone else's life? The Bible is the living word of God; it is not just a history book! Larry and I have NOT done anything that each of you cannot do by simply BELIEVING that God is FAITHFUL to fulfill ALL His PROMISES, and He has actually put them in writing and vowed it in His own Son's blood!!!

You can open your mouth and your heart and do what God has created you to do; talk to Him.

Joyfully His,
Larry & Stacie

Chapter 3

ॐ

May 4, 2008
Subject: We Danced for an Hour

Hello Everyone,

On Friday Larry and I received a very precious gift. The Physical Therapy staff set up Larry's Frankenstein table in a separate but adjoining room in the therapy department, and when he reached 90 degrees they put on Frank Sinatra and gave us some space. I put his arms over my shoulders and just hugged and swayed with my eyes closed while cherishing and memorizing this sweet place in time. It was an amazing sensation that I didn't think that I would ever feel again, then he topped it off by initiating kisses! The time passed so quickly and before we knew it he had tolerated 60 minutes of standing. What a spectacular experience!

Our prayer for each of you this week is that you count your time with your spouse as precious. We want to encourage you to perpetuate a premeditated act of kindness and create a special memory for your spouse or a family member. Life is too brief to hold a grudge or to take the ones that we love the most for granted. Please plan to create a special memory this week. We promise that you will not regret it.

"*Love is patient, love is kind. It does not envy, it does not boast, it is not proud. Love is not rude, it is not self-seeking, it is not easily angered, and it keeps no record of wrongs. Love does not delight in evil, but rejoices with the truth. It always trusts, always hopes, always protects, and always perseveres. Love NEVER fails!*" 1 Corinthians 13:4-8.

A preacher once taught me to put my name in the blank instead of the word love whenever I was tempted to operate in the flesh, and he assured me that my love walk would develop rapidly. He was right, it really did cause me to act in love toward those people that I professed to love, but took for granted, spoke rudely to or was impatient with.

Joyfully His,
Larry & Stacie

May 16, 2008
Hello Everybody,

Larry comes home on May 22nd and we are feverishly making all of the preparations. He has made some great advances in his ability to communicate and to use his hands, but I will still require a special lift to get him in and out of bed on my own.

Because Larry is being discharged under a home health program instead of hospice rules (they are significantly different), I am scrambling like a mad woman to accommodate all the changes. The amount of physical support alone will be cut by 66 to 75 percent right off the bat. The good news is that while Larry has been in the residential rehab facility I have been going to the gym to build my strength as well as some serious Bible studies and prayer to sustain my faith.

Without a battle there can be no victory. Impossible is one of God's favorite words. For every adversity there is a seed of equal or greater opportunity. We are ready and looking forward to the next chapter in this life adventure that our God has entrusted us to walk on perfect faith in His promises.

Joyfully His,
Larry & Stacie

May 30, 2008
Subject: Home & Gone Again

Hello Everyone,

Larry came home on May 22nd, and we were just starting to find a routine when he developed a high fever that could not be controlled and had to be hospitalized on May 27th.

Yesterday marked seven months since Larry came back from the dead, and we spent our day in introspection. We asked questions like: What are we doing with our lives to benefit God? Are we doing what God wants for our lives? What can we do to bless others using the time, circumstances and resources that we have?

It occurred to me that the only reason that we exist at all is because God created us to live in these mortal bodies temporarily. We were created by and for God to be His family. This terrestrial existence is simply our proving ground for our eternal destiny. It is vitally important to maintain this perspective especially when you feel like you are fighting dragons. When you are up to your neck in alligators, it is hard to remember that your objective was to drain the swamp! But our God has not left us defenseless. He has given us *the shield of faith with which we may quench ALL the fiery darts of the wicked one*. (Ephesians 6:16)

Our whole purpose for living is to love and please our Heavenly Father, so why do we make it so complicated and even foolishly try to be our own god by worrying or being depressed as if that will change anything?

If I claim to be a child of God, then I must bear fruit that is consistent with being repentant. (Luke 3:8)

Because every tree that does not bear good fruit is cut down and thrown into the fire. (Luke 3:9)

Bearing good fruit means to go out and put my faith in God into action by doing something that helps people even if there is risk involved. Bearing good fruit means to take my eyes off of myself and my own desires and put them on the needs of others. Jesus said, *"Whoever of you desires to be first shall be servant to all."* (Mark 10:44)

Larry and I thank you for your continued prayers for his restoration, and we thank God for each of you daily.

Joyfully His,
Larry & Stacie

June 12, 2008
Subject: More Adventures

Hello Everybody,

Larry came home from the Naval Hospital on June 2nd and has been receiving physical, occupational, and speech therapy, as well as extensive wound care for his bed sores. My days have been totally consumed with his care and therapy schedule. I continue to covet your prayers for us to meet every gauntlet with love and peace.

Yesterday while his nurse was here he started running a temperature and his doctor said to bring him to the ER. Upon arrival his temp was 104. Yes, they kept him last night. I expect him to come home today or tomorrow.

No matter what struggles you may be enduring today, it is vital that you maintain an eternal perspective in order to function effectively and not fall into the enemy's trap of depression. Always remember that Satan is a liar and the father of all lies and the truth is not in him!

For I consider that the sufferings of this present time are not worthy to be compared with the glory, which shall be revealed in us. (Romans 8:18) This verse has been of immeasurable value to me in keeping my life and temporary circumstances in the correct perspective. Larry and I want to encourage each of you to memorize this simple verse and thereby store it away in your heart to give you great strength and perseverance when you encounter struggles.

Joyfully His,
Larry & Stacie

June 17, 2008
Subject: My Honey is Home

Hello Everyone,

Larry came home from the hospital last night. Just to recap, he was admitted to the Naval Hospital on the 11th with a temperature of 104, which turned out to be a urinary tract infection. He spiked another temp on Thursday that precluded him coming home on Friday. Then his right thigh swelled up so they started treating him for a blood clot. Yesterday, the ultrasound confirmed that he has at least one blood clot in his right calf, but that does not explain the huge swelling in the right thigh. He is in a bit of pain but is still able to give kisses and repeat I love you.

So this week's new skill set for me includes giving Larry daily injections (for the next three to six months) to dissolve the blood clot. I am sure that all of the practical hands on training I have received while taking care of Larry will be put to good use when I return to Kenya next year to minister to orphans that are HIV positive. The Lord has given my friend Laura the vision to look after the most despised, dejected and hopeless human beings on the planet, and she has asked me to go with her.

From the fruit of his lips a man is filled with good things as surely as the work of his hands rewards him. (Proverbs 12:14)

Reckless words pierce like a sword, but the tongue of the wise brings healing. (Proverbs 12:18)

He who guards his lips guards his life, but he who speaks rashly will come to ruin. (Proverbs 13:3)

No matter your resources, my God will honor ANY effort that you make to bless others, even minding your tongue. I guarantee that if you take your eyes off of yourself and put them on others that you will never be depressed. There are always people in greater need than you.

We love you guys more than we can express. Thank you for your generous prayers.

Joyfully His,
Larry & Stacie

June 29, 2008
Subject: Still Interesting

Hi Everyone,

This week has been very problematic. Well actually, the whole month has been that way, but at least we are not bored. Remember when Larry was discharged from the hospital on the 16th and he still had an unexplainable swelling in his right thigh that could not be attributed to the confirmed blood clot in the same calf? Well, they expected the swelling to go down as a result of the daily blood thinner injections, but it actually got worse. So the doctor called Wednesday morning to have me bring him to the hospital to run more tests, and they ended up keeping Larry overnight.

The good news is that he does not have any cancer in his abdomen (or elsewhere), and he does not have any additional blood clots. The blood flow is actually being somewhat restricted by the formation of bone in the thigh muscle. It is yet another medical mystery, and there is no treatment for it.

Last time I wrote I spoke about depression. Please understand that I am preaching to myself as well as keeping our friends informed. There is a huge difference between feeling sad and being depressed. The medical profession has a long list of acceptable reasons for people being depressed, and although Larry and I qualify as eligible in multiple categories, we have not given in. You may ask why? It is not that Larry or I am any better than anyone else, and it is not that God likes us better than anyone else or that we have earned special powers by being super spiritual. It is not even because we are so mentally tough that we are able to live on the edge of life for months on end without cracking up. No, it is because we love and trust God completely. What kind of hypocrites would we be if we called ourselves Christians (believers in Jesus as the promised Messiah) but had no faith, hope or trust in our Savior, Redeemer and Creator?

In the last few weeks I have been pretty stressed and frustrated and my joy had ebbed. There has been a significant increase in my workload, but I expected to maintain the same standards. When I failed, I became discouraged and actually had a major meltdown last Sunday where I just could not stop sobbing. In the final analysis it was not the extra work that tripped me up, it was that I wanted to see Larry get better as a result of my efforts, and I was greatly disappointed. It goes right back to the question of being a Christian or a hypocrite. I know the joy of the Lord is my strength, and that it is impossible to please God without faith. So it is a forgone conclusion that I was doomed to be disappointed, because I failed to trust my Heavenly Father to do what only God can do.

It is funny to look back now and see that I thought God needed my help, but it is an insidious trap. I have a propensity for pushing forward at full force to accomplish any perceived mission. This is both a strength as well as a weakness. Lord, how I miss Larry's counter balance in my life!

So if you run into some extra challenges this week, you can save yourself a lot of grief by doing your best, and allowing God to be God and do His part just as He has promised.

Joyfully His,
Larry & Stacie

July 7, 2008
Subject: Nearly One Year Ago

Hi Everyone,

I find myself at peace and in my right mind as I realize that I am so not looking to medical science for any further help in Larry's restorative process. I have a to-do list of things each day that can be quite daunting even if Larry's tummy is having a good day. If I were trying to do all of this in my own strength instead of the supernatural power of God, I would have been toast months ago.

Larry and I are in a very unique position in that we literally have no other options except to trust God. None of the medicine or therapy or procedures are capable of restoring Larry, only God can do that. It made me laugh just now when I remembered a conversation that took place between Jesus and Peter where Jesus told his disciples (perhaps 100 of them) that if they did not drink his blood and eat his flesh that they could not be his disciples and a bunch of them left. Then Jesus turned to the twelve and asked if they wanted to leave also, to which his home boy Peter replied, "Yo man, like you are the alpha and omega, the Son of God, Creator of the universe of everything seen and unseen, our Savior and Messiah, - duh, have you lost your mind? Where else could we go? Who in the world could we possibly trust besides you?" Now obviously that is my very heavily embellished paraphrase of John 6:53-68, but it serves as an excellent summary for our faith walk during this year of testing. There is no place or person or any amount of science that can remotely compare to the powerful love and immutable promises of our God for His children.

Blessed is the man who trusts in the Lord, and whose hope is in the Lord. For he shall be like a tree planted by the river, and will not fear when heat comes; but its leaf will be green, and will not be anxious in the year of drought, nor will it cease in yielding fruit. (Jeremiah 17:78)

The 12th of July will make one year since (Larry was diagnosed with cancer) our ordeal began, and although we cannot say that we have not had some anxious moments, we can say they were just that—moments. We have been sustained during our year of drought by the living water of Jesus Christ, and there is no other possible explanation.

"Prayer will bring change to the person praying, not to God." ~ Dr. Wayne Skinner

Prayer truly is a marvelous mystery and I have seen it manifest in many of you as you have cheered us on and interceded on our behalf. No amount of plastic surgery can bring about such a change in countenance as a prayer-filled heart. We appreciate each of you so much.

Joyfully His,
Larry & Stacie

July 17, 2008
Subject: A Beautiful Thing

Hello Everybody,

Two weeks ago a friend of mine who I really got to know during a mission trip to Africa asked if there were any tasks that she could do for me, and I let her know that I had a painting project that I needed help with. So, I now have white trim and eves on my house instead of carnival ride blue! We were able to do two coats in one day, and after we finished, she admitted that she was afraid of heights and spiders, but she fearlessly faced both in order to help me do a project that I could not have done by myself. What a beautiful thing.

My daughter-in-law has been staying with Larry each morning this week so that I could volunteer at Vacation Bible School. Her effort has enabled me to minister to three kids from our neighborhood so they can have some fun and learn about Jesus. What a beautiful thing.

I will be going to North Carolina this weekend on a business trip and a friend of ours who is a Navy nurse has volunteered to take care of my Larry. What a beautiful thing.

From Monday to Thursday next week I will be in Washington, D.C., for the Christians United for Israel Summit and a friend who is a certified nursing assistant is taking time off from work so that she can work for Larry. What a beautiful thing.

When I look around at the state of the world I know that it will not be much longer now and Jesus will return for His Church without blemish or wrinkle. What a beautiful thing. Maybe we better get ready?

Larry seems very happy and he gets a little better every day. What a beautiful thing.

Joyfully His,
Larry & Stacie

July 18, 2008
Subject: More Beauty

Hello Everyone,

A man dressed as Jesus appeared in the sanctuary during Vacation Bible School today and upon seeing him, my little five-year-old friend, was so excited to see him that he ran right up to Jesus, hugged Him and told Jesus that he loved Him. I saw Jesus get a big lump in his throat, and then he bent down and whispered something to my little friend. What a beautiful thing.

During our drive home my young friend said, "Do you know what Jesus whispered to me? He said that I should not hit my brothers or sisters and that they should not hit me and we should love each other." What a beautiful thing.

Actually to quote Jesus from Matthew 22: 37-39, He said, *"LOVE THE LORD YOUR GOD WITH ALL YOUR HEART AND WITH ALL OUR SOUL AND WITH ALL YOUR MIND. THIS IS THE FIRST AND GREATEST COMMANDMENT. AND THE SECOND IS LIKE IT: LOVE YOUR NEIGHBOR AS YOURSELF. Everything in life pivots on these two commandments.* What a beautiful thing.

There has never been a statue erected to a critic. Of all of the callings and gifts listed in the Bible there is no such gifting as criticism. Critical words wound much deeper and with more intense, far flung aftershocks than any physical damage could inflict. Can you imagine what a beautiful thing it would be in the eyes of God to see His children getting along with one another?

My Mother's favorite saying was, "Charity begins at home." If you cannot be loving toward the people you profess to love (but who also get on your nerves the most), then acting loving toward strangers is just a phony facade. What a beautiful thing it would be to practice charity at home and let it spill over into and onto the rest of our lives.

Joyfully His,
Larry & Stacie

August 15, 2008
Subject: All Things Are Possible

Hello Everybody,

Wow, it has been a while since my last update and I do not mean to worry any of you. Everything has been going quite well actually as evidenced by the fact that Larry has been home in my full-time care for over a month. He has made some remarkable strides in fine muscle movement and dexterity. Yes, Mr. "Happy Hands" now regularly disconnects, pulls out, or plays with everything he can reach. These spectacular catastrophes have really kept me busy. Please do not misunderstand I would not exchange any of these inconvenient mishaps for the progress that he has made.

Matthew, Larry and I will be leaving tomorrow for the Great Lakes Believer's Convention in Milwaukee, Wisconsin. This will be a week of soaking in the anointing of God and intense immersion training in the Bible. Yes, it is an enormous undertaking, but we have never been afraid of a little adventure.

Don't be afraid, but only believe that with God all things are possible.

Joyfully His,
Larry & Stacie

August 17, 2008
Subject: Delayed but Undaunted

Hello Everyone,

Instead of leaving for Wisconsin yesterday we went to the ER because Larry had been having explosive diarrhea for 24 hours. They plumped him up with a bag of saline and gave me a new prescription on top of the antibiotics that I have been giving him.

Finally, be strong with the Lord's mighty power. Put on all of God's armor so that you will be able to stand firm against all strategies and tricks of the Devil. For we are not fighting against people made of flesh and blood, but against evil rulers and authorities of the unseen world, against those mighty powers of darkness who rule this world, and against wicked spirits in the heavenly realms. Use every piece of God's armor to resist the enemy in the time of evil, so that after the battle you will still be standing firm. Stand your ground, putting on the sturdy belt of truth and the body armor of God's righteousness. For shoes put on the peace that comes from the Good News, so that you will be fully prepared. I every battle you will need faith as your shield to stop the fiery arrows aimed at you by Satan. Put on salvation as your helmet, and take the sword of the Spirit, which is the word of God. Pray at all times and on every occasion in the power of the Holy Spirit. Stay alert and be persistent in your prayers for all Christians everywhere. (Ephesians 6:10-18 NLT)

This is how we ask each of you to pray and intercede on our behalf as we go on this journey to actively grow in our relationship with our Savior Jesus Christ.

Larry, Matthew and I will be leaving at 4 a.m. tomorrow.

Joyfully His,
Larry & Stacie

August 28, 2008
Subject: Home Again

Hi Everyone,

Wow, what an adventure! We were on our way home from Wisconsin when I realized that the only reason this trip was such a smashing success was that none of us realized that it was impossible. We got home late Sunday night with an odometer reading of 2,077 miles.

I only thought I was ready for such a trip, but it was well worth the mental, emotional and physical exertion to make such an epic journey.

The most worthwhile and inspiring part of this trip was the amazing unity of the Body of Christ in loving heartfelt worship by people of every imaginable denominational background from all over the world. There is no way to explain the intimacy of praising God in the midst of thousands of strangers who are in agreement and uninhibited because of anonymity. It is a rush that I cannot duplicate in my personal prayer or praise and worship time with God. There is tremendous joy and encouragement in the unified corporate fellowship of Believers.

As a result of this time away with God we have returned home completely refreshed and strengthened in our resolve to live our lives (regardless of the circumstances) full force for God. I am reminded that every morning as I open my eyes that God has essentially hit the restart button on the computer program of my life. I get to start fresh each day and give it my all. Anne Sullivan (Helen Keller's teacher) sums this up perfectly, "Keep on beginning and failing. Each time you fail, start all over again, and you will grow stronger until you have accomplished a purpose. Not the one you began with perhaps, but one you'll be glad to remember."

We love each of you so much and gratefully thank God for your friendship.

Joyfully His,
Larry & Stacie

Chapter 4

ॐ

October 5, 2008
Subject: Off the Radar

Hello Everybody,

S orry for being off of the radar for a bit longer than I should have been, but we have been undergoing such a wonderful transformation that our days have just zipped by.

Since we returned from our spiritual journey/vacation we have both approached our lives in a new perspective that is making a huge difference. Larry's movements have become much more controlled and significantly less spastic. His tactile defensiveness is dramatically reduced. He is swallowing a larger variety of foods at the same pace that anyone would. His physical strength improves daily and his stamina has improved to the point of being able to stand with my assistance for a full hour at a time. He is now able to mimic numerous one syllable words. He is able to turn pages in photo albums and express recognition for specific individuals. He is able to grab onto things and then let go on command. He is now able to balance himself while lying on his side for up to an hour at a time. He is clearly able to express himself through his emotions, and his heart melting smile is returning. This week we are going to start coloring with big crayons. Larry's overall health has improved to the point that he is as stable as anyone. He is off of all medications except a blood thinner. His bed sores are continuing to heal but still require cleaning and dressing two to three times per day. Oh, and we are going to attempt a toilet program also. We did have to make an ER visit a couple weeks ago to clear up a urinary tract infection as a result of the permanent catheter. His tube feeding has been reduced to five cans a day because of his ability to consume more calories orally. Now with all of this increased capability, treatments and therapy, I have been as busy as a long tailed cat in a room full of rocking chairs.

Please forgive me for not writing sooner, I did not mean to worry anyone. In this case though no news truly was good news, and I have been basking in the glory of it all.

The therapeutic assistance that we receive under a home health care program is significantly restricted as opposed to residential rehab. On the other hand being in a nursing home can easily be summed up as human warehousing experience.

I am so thankful for the Internet! I was actually able to find a recipe for a wound cleansing concoction that I am able to prepare fresh daily in my kitchen as opposed to special ordering three bottles a week through a pharmacy for lots of money.

Just to reinforce how outstanding all of this progress is; please keep in mind that just by breathing on his own Larry defies all expectations of medical science. According to Larry's diagnosis, his progress is absolutely impossible. That is why we are so grateful that, nothing is impossible with God. We can do all things through Christ Jesus who strengthens us, and according to Jesus, we are more than conquerors! This is why I am able to leap out of bed each morning in wild expectation for the miracles I see my Heavenly Daddy performing in Larry every day.

Joyfully His,
Larry & Stacie

October 16, 2008
Subject: Singing Along

Hello Everybody,

Wow, it has been almost two weeks since our last update and so much has happened!

We have a nurses' aide that comes twice a week and she is just a gifted lady that takes extra time to teach Larry a new word each time. But even better than being able to mimic words, he is now able to respond to the question, "What is your name?" Often with varying degrees of clarity but usually it is crystal clear and unmistakable! Being able to say his own name is yet another milestone on this miracle journey.

We have a new machine that is literally sucking his wounds shut. It is called a wound vacuum, so hopefully by Christmas we will be wound free.

Larry's favorite song has always been "Yes, Jesus Loves Me," and while singing it to him this week, he started to sing along. Now you would never be able to identify it by naming that tune, but at least he recognized it and mumbled along.

Larry has a new doctor that is part of a consortium called "Physicians for Homebound Patients." She is very thorough and spent nearly two hours here on the initial visit. What a miraculous blessing to find a doctor that makes house calls.

"DID I NOT SAY TO YOU THAT IF YOU WOULD BELIEVE YOU WOULD SEE THE GLORY OF GOD?" -JESUS (John 11: 40)

May all of you see the glory of God no matter how adverse the circumstances appear in the world of economics, politics, environment or your personal situations and relationships.

Joyfully His,
Larry & Stacie

October 29, 2008
Subject: One Year

Hi Everyone,

Yes, one year ago today Larry passed out in our kitchen and died for 23 minutes. I can honestly say that it has been the slowest and fastest and most intense year of my life. Today has been an emotional day to say the least.

Two things have enabled me to get through this year— God and people. By God I mean keeping everything in an eternal perspective and maintaining constant communication with Him. The people that I am referring to are those of you who have befriended us and continued to uplift us and bathe us in prayer, which is the most precious gift we could ask for.

He will wipe away every tear from their eyes; and there will no longer be any death; there will no longer be any mourning, or crying or pain. (Revelation 21:4)

Joyfully His,
Larry & Stacie

November 14, 2008
Subject: More Progress

Hi Everybody,

Well, this has been a very eventful two weeks to say the least. On November third Larry was able to correctly execute his first command. As part of his speech therapy, he receives some oral food and he was able to open his mouth in response to the word bite or open wide. Previously he was only able to get his eyebrows to go up because the neuropathway was not correctly routed to his mouth. This is a really big deal even though it may sound weird. Imagine someone talking to you and you can't get the message to the right part of your body to respond. Okay, here is the really important part: medical science says that this is impossible after all of this time, so the only explanation is that God is recreating and reconnecting the circuitry in Larry's brain.

November 10th I received an urgent phone call because my son Matthew had passed out in the shower and fallen face first on the floor. He was lying in such a position that his body was blocking the door, which meant the EMTs wound up ramming the door open repeatedly against his ribs in order to get to him. Of course, this only added more trauma to his injuries. I drove his wife to the emergency room and after about five anxious hours and a number of tests, it was determined that he was suffering from severe exhaustion coupled with a sudden drop in blood pressure by going straight from the Jacuzzi tub into the shower. It is only by the grace and protection of God that Matthew was not more grossly or permanently injured as a result of the way he fell.

On November 12th while doing a dressing change on one of Larry's bed sores, his nurse discovered something too grotesque and graphic for me to describe in this letter. As a result of this discovery, compounded with the knowledge that he was probably fighting two other infections, I took him to the Naval Hospital ER on the 13th. He was admitted for further observation, and I believe for my peace of mind.

I am so grateful for God's provision of just the right people and support at just the right moment in time. Without

Him I would have been certifiable long ago! Larry and I are so appreciative of all of the love and kindness that each of you has shown to us, and we reciprocate by praying for you always. I want to challenge each of you to have the courage to trust God completely and to talk with Him openly and honestly about every intimate detail in your life because He is faithful. The alternative for me would be depression, emptiness, frustration and insanity.

Joyfully His,
Larry & Stacie

November 17, 2008
Subject: A Journal Entry

Hello Everyone,

I have been asked to share a highly sensitive journal conversation with each of you. Due to the large number of people on this list and the many divergent backgrounds, I am sure some of you will be blessed by this message, while others will be offended. For that reason I am asking you in advance to take the grocery store approach: If there is something on the shelves that you do not need or that you are not ready for, just leave it there and go on your way peacefully.

Lord, do I only love You because You are my last hope? Do I pretend to love you because You are all that I have and the only One that I can count on? Do I only love You out of desperation? Do I only love You because it is the "right" thing to do? Oh God, how demeaning and hurtful that would be to You.

Please forgive me Lord if that is how I have made You feel. I am so sorry. You deserve so much more than to be my last bastion, because it is the logical choice as everyone else and everything in life has failed me. You and I both know that I can count on no one but You. But that is true regardless of the situations in our lives. This is really TRUTH! You are FAITHFUL and LOYAL to Your creation.

God, I want to be a blessing to You. God, I want to please You and bring You joy and pure love.

You are not my course of last resort. You Lord God are my first choice, my love and my hearts' desire above all things or people. You Lord are my great reward and lover and best friend. Forgive me for acting as if You were a consolation prize because my life was in the sewer, and I had nowhere else to turn so I gave my attention to You.

God, You alone are worthy of all my love and respect and honor. Please help me stay focused on Your goodness.

I will meditate on the glorious splendor of Your majesty, and on Your wondrous works. (Psalms 145:5)

My mouth shall speak the praise of the Lord, and all flesh shall bless His holy name forever and ever. Praise the Lord. Praise the Lord, O my soul. While I live I will praise the Lord; I will sing praises to my God while I have my being. (Psalms 145:20-146:2)

Please forgive me Lord for acting downtrodden with false humility. I am not trudging through life depending on people, possessions or money as my god. You, Lord are the one true, living, victorious Creator of all things seen and unseen. How dare I act as if You are finite or self-focused! You are my glorious, incomprehensible, loving God and Daddy. I am only capable of love because You loved me first, and while I was still a sinner, You sent Your only begotten Son to die for me and to pay the price for my sin by going to Hell in my place.

Thank You Lord for Your great mercy and patience with me. Please help me to remain focused and prioritized on those things that are important to You. Help me to block out the noise and pressures of the world and to walk in perfect faith and love toward You and for all mankind, in Jesus' Name I pray. Amen.

I love you guys and I hope that my embarrassment and open confession will benefit each of you in developing an intimate relationship (two way conversation) with our Creator.

Joyfully His,
Stacie

November 22, 2008
Subject: 100 Days Begins

Hello Everybody,

It has been one bodacious roller coaster filled week! I don't have a clue how I would have negotiated the challenges without my total trust in the omnipotent Creator of the universe. So, I am going to drastically simplify this by stating the bottom line: Larry was transferred from the hospital to a rehabilitation facility yesterday, where he is authorized to spend the next 100 days.

In recent history I have had more than one man of the cloth try to convince me that it is okay to be mad at God because He can handle it. While I am sure that is true, God also has feelings and feelings can be hurt. So let's take this out of the theoretical realm and into the practical. When you are mad at someone, you are not open to genuine communication, and you are certainly not walking in love or forgiveness. Children get mad at parents all of the time, because their parents do not agree with their selfish or foolish desires.

Of course, I have been disappointed with some of the events in our lives, but God is the only being that loves me unconditionally and in Whom I can trust completely. It would be the epitome of stupidity for me to be angry with Him. It has also been my observation that being mad at God will plunge you into the pit of absolute despair. Unforgiveness and anger work together, and will eat you alive as surely as any cancer. Oh, and by the way, there is nothing in the "owners' manual" that says it is okay to be mad at anyone, let alone at God.

Larry and I are praying for people who are experiencing depression. We are praying that they will cast all of their fears, worries and heartaches over on their awesome Creator and loving Daddy. Unity of prayer brings about great transformation. Would you join us this week in praying for the deliverance of desperate and depressed people both generally and specifically?

May we all be grateful in counting our many blessings and giving thanks to God this Thursday.

Joyfully His,
Larry & Stacie

November 30, 2008
Subject: Thanksgiving Update

Merry Thanksgiving Everyone,

Larry has settled into his new digs finally, and he was very cheerful this afternoon. As a matter of fact, Larry was very clearly communicating appropriately with head nods and shakes today. Visiting hours are from 8 a.m. to 8 p.m. daily.

While Larry was still at the Naval Hospital, one of the nurses emphasized to us just how much of a miracle it is that

Larry still alive! She explained that in order to be considered a successful resuscitation, the individual must survive at least 24 hours. The percentage of people who accomplish that feat is only one percent! But even of the successful resuscitations, most of them do not survive seven days, let alone more than a year like Larry. I was shocked to hear these statistics, but encouraged to have a health care professional spontaneously acknowledge the undeniable divine intervention in Larry's life.

For most of us it is easier to give heartfelt thanks in some years; and in others we need to push ourselves to find and remember exactly what it is we are truly thankful for. Today we are living in a time of great uncertainty, and you may be among those who are asking yourself, "What do I have to be truly thankful for?"

Let us make three suggestions. First, we should all share in thanks that God loves each one of us and longs to be in a relationship with us. Second, we can be thankful that we live in a time and place where we can worship openly and publicly proclaim our love and allegiance to the Lord. Finally, whether the Lord has blessed us with much or little, He has blessed us with enough to share with someone in need, who needs to be reminded and encouraged of His love.

Whenever I am tempted to throw myself a pity party, I look around and see so many people who are worse off than we are, and I thank God for His mercy, miracles and love.

Joyfully His,
Larry & Stacie

December 22, 2008
Subject: Christmas Approaches

Hi Everyone,

Only three days until Christmas and all is well. Larry is progressing daily, and he is very happy. Last night our Sunday School Class threw a party in his room and sang Christmas carols.

On December 26, Larry will be going to De Paul Medical Center to have one of his wounds surgically altered. This should help him heal faster.

The neighborhood Christmas Caroling adventure was a huge success and a very surprising blessing to all involved.

This Christmas season has been one of reaching remarkable new heights in love and generosity. We have collaborated in numerous outreach projects and supported more ministries than ever before. I am reminded every day that God himself has prepared good works for us to do long before we were even conceived.

I am also reminded of a teaching that helps me practice love by inserting my name into every spot that the word love appears in 1 Corinthians 13. Since I can think of no greater gift to give each of you than love; I am sending this so you can insert your name in the blanks. You may want to print it and use it to grow more like Jesus in your character and actions.

_____ is patient, _____ is kind. I do not envy, I do not boast, I am not proud. I am not rude, I am not self-seeking, I am not easily angered, I keep no record of wrongs. _____ does not delight in evil but rejoices with the truth. I always trust, always hope, always protect, always persevere. With the love of God I cannot fail!

Larry and I love and appreciate you more than you will ever know.

Joyfully His,
Larry & Stacie

December 29, 2008
Subject: Back in the ER

Hi Everybody,

1. Larry went to a special wound care clinic on Friday and received a very thorough evaluation, but they were not able to do any surgical debreedment at that time for a number of reasons that I will not explain now.
2. Saturday night when I went to visit Larry at the rehabilitation facility/nursing home, I was alarmed over a very large swollen area on his right upper arm. The nurse at the facility called the doctor and was instructed to have Larry taken to the ER. We went to Portsmouth Naval where everyone knows him and all his medical history is on the computer. Larry was admitted to the hospital and is receiving massive antibiotics.
3. I am grateful that every time I am faced with a lethal threat on Larry's life that the promises of God (that I have hidden away in my heart) perk up and carry me through even the most sinister of circumstances. My bedrock promise that I rely upon most is: *"I WILL NEVER LEAVE YOU OR FORSAKE YOU."* - Jesus
4. Larry and I are thankful for all of your faith filled prayers on our behalf, as we also continue to pray for each of you. We pray that each of you remember the words of Jesus (Matthew 24) concerning the end times; that you may be His beacon of light to a fearful and confused world during 2009.

Joyfully His,
Larry & Stacie

January 5, 2009
Subject: A New Year

Hi Everyone,

Happy New Year to all our dear friends who have become our family!

Last Tuesday (12-30-08) we received a true Christmas miracle when Larry was discharged from the hospital into the premier rehabilitation facility in all of Hampton Roads! Of course this did not happen without a tumultuous ordeal, but our God is bigger than any bureaucratic system. Again Larry would not even be alive if not for God's divine intervention. The baseball size lump on Larry's arm remains an unsolved mystery, but it has dissolved in response to massive antibiotics.

You KNOW that the devil has come only to steal, kill and destroy. But Jesus has come to destroy the works of the devil and to give us life more abundantly. You KNOW that the devil is our enemy; not people, institutions or broken systems. You also KNOW that no renegade angel or any of his demons can defeat our Heavenly Father who is the Creator of all things, so as long as we remain in faith toward Him; we cannot be defeated either!

I have been given the opportunity to practice a little bit of "Larry Wisdom" by not writing a full report condemning or criticizing what happened with him. (No gory details.) Instead, I am free to pray for all the people involved and for a change in the socialistic system that breeds such an environment. Truly the best revenge is to love and to pray for those who spitefully use us!

Let me remind each of you that it is because of your faithful prayers that we are lifted up. Thank you for all of your love, commitment and support.

Joyfully His,
Stacie & Larry
January 9, 2009
Subject: Journal Entry

God, You have made us (mankind) righteous through the blood of Your Son Jesus. I am Your righteous instrument of love on this planet. I love being a tool in Your hand.

The righteousness of God is through faith in Jesus Christ, to all and on all who believe. (Romans 3:22)

Thank You Jesus for redeeming us and making us the righteous implements of God almighty.

But let all those rejoice who put their trust in You; let them ever shout for joy, because You defend them; let those also who love Your name be joyful in You. For You, O Lord, will bless the righteous; with favor, You will surround him as with a shield. (Psalm 5:11-12)

Isaac continued to sow seed even during drought and famine. Thank You Lord for giving us such a generous hearts to continue sowing into the lives of others even in such harsh circumstances.

Wow, thank You so much for Your love, protection, joy and righteousness God! We love You.

Life is a university, so I go to school every day.

January 14, 2009
Subject: Journal Entry

Thy will be done, Thy Kingdom come...NOW.

Here I am, send me Lord. I will do ANYTHING That You ask! Here I am Lord, use me to accomplish Your will on earth just as it is in Heaven.

I work and struggle, using Christ's great strength that works so powerfully in me. (Colossians 1:29)

Thank You Lord for opening the eyes of my heart to see You so clearly. Thank You for allowing me to peek over into another realm or dimension that my physical mind cannot begin to comprehend, but that my spiritual mind yearns for. Let me use every resource that You have placed in me to benefit all of mankind. Expand my mind to see the possibilities (endless possibilities) that You have put at my disposal.

Jesus help me to study Your earthly life and implement all that You exemplify. I am a Jesus follower. Jesus I pray for every denomination that calls themselves "Christians" to seek You and to imitate You Jesus, completely. I pray Lord that we in the body of Christ would be strengthened in love and unified in love to bless one another and to grow as individuals in Your Army.

January 19, 2009
Subject: Journal Entry

Thank you Lord for showing me that mankind's obsession with building houses, mansions and palaces is based upon our need to feel safe, protected and secure in a compartmentalized collection of specialized categories. It is in our very DNA that You have programmed us to desire individuality while in community, like specialization of cells in an organ and organs in the body. We are supernaturally driven to seek a home, family and commonality of cause. We are called to each do our part in the body of Christ.

"In My Father's house there are many mansions, I go to prepare a place for each of you." ~ Jesus

Our spirits are eternal and God specifically designed and created us to be part of His Son Jesus. We crave to live in big houses in the nicest neighborhoods now because it is ingrained in our makeup from our conception, but it is the eternal mansion that we are actually seeking and trying to achieve for ourselves. Our in-born yearning can be construed as an earthly goal instead of an eternal destination.

January 22, 2009
Subject: Larry is Talking Again

Hello Everybody,

I am glad to report that Larry has started to talk again, but I do not always understand what he is saying. My favorite of course is "I love you," which I do understand. He was way too sick to speak at all for the past three weeks. Although he has had a serious setback, we expect him to recover the previously conquered skills.

"Character cannot be developed in ease and quiet. Only through experiences of trial and suffering can the soul be strengthened, vision cleared, ambition inspired and success achieved." ~Helen Keller

"You find out who you are in your moments of greatest disappointment." ~Robert Kiyosaki (Author of Rich Dad, Poor Dad)

Each of us experience setbacks and disappointments in our lives, and it is all part of the journey. But these things do not have to rob you of joy and love. Each one of us was put on this planet for a specific purpose, and none of us can accomplish our destiny alone. We need each other. Our love and joy cannot be stripped from us as long as we remain focused on our Creator and love one another as He commanded. Unity and joy are the result of love. I have seen God weave a beautiful tapestry in all of our lives as you have ministered to us and we have minister to you.

Larry and I have experienced two cataclysmic events and endured protracted sorrow only by and through the love of God and the unity of our family in Christ Jesus. Part of Larry's destiny is to positively impact thousands of lives because of his example in imitating Jesus. Each of us has benefited from walking with Jesus through Larry's struggles.

We ask each of you to remain unified in faith for Larry's complete restoration, in Jesus' Name.

Joyfully His,
Stacie & Larry

January 25, 2009
Subject: Journal Entry

I love You Lord first and foremost in my life. Thank You for showing me how Jesus came and lived as a man. *"But [Christ Jesus] made himself of no reputation, and took upon himself the form of a servant, and was made in the likeness of men."* (Philippians 2:7) This means that I can and should aspire to live just like Jesus. Jesus, You are our example for living a good and righteous life before our Father.

January 27, 2009
Subject: Another Setback

Hello Everyone,

Well we have had a little set back this week in that Larry spiked a pretty high temperature, but the good news is that he is in the right place to receive instant corrective measures. More good news is that Larry continues to speak to me and responds appropriately to simple yes and no questions. But we have experienced a supernatural mode of communication, which is totally unexplainable.

Some of you have wondered how we stay so motivated and positive all of the time. I found a passage while doing my devotions that sums this up very well.

So we're not giving up. How could we! Even though on the outside it often looks like things are falling apart on us, on the inside, God is making new life, not a day goes by without His unfolding grace. These hard times are small potatoes compared to the coming good times, the lavish celebration prepared for us. There's far more than meets the eye. The things we see now are here today, gone tomorrow. But the things we can't see now will last forever. For instance, we know that when these bodies of ours are taken down like tents and folded away, they will be replaced by resurrection bodies in heaven; God-made, not handmade. (2 Corinthians 4:16-5:1 Message Bible)

I just finished reading an amazing book, "90 Minutes in Heaven," by Don Piper. It is the account of a man who was clinically dead (like Larry) and what he experienced. It's a must read in my opinion if only for the heart quickening description of heaven.

Joyfully His,
Larry & Stacie

February 6, 2009
Subject: Journal Entry

Lord, You alone guide me through a difficult maze of situations and decisions. You provide EVERYTHING that I need to bring glory and honor to Your Name.

Thank You, Lord for loving me so well. You are an awesome Daddy!

February 7, 2009
Subject: Journal Entry

God, I don't know why I have been so emotional and crying for two days. I have felt totally isolated and alone. I have no human being to trust or lean on. I am all alone and extremely lonely. Please strengthen me and hold me close to Your heart, as I walk through this valley. Please don't take this as ungratefulness, but I need Larry back at full strength. I am so tired. Please help us Lord. Our hope has been deferred for 15 months; longer if we count from July 12, 2007 with the Leukemia struggle.

What do You want from me God? What have I failed to do? What am I doing wrong? Whatever You want from me, I am eager to do or give!

I love You and I know You love me and You love Larry. We cannot begin to comprehend how much You love us. We know that all of this calamity is not Your desire for Your children. I am thankful that Larry and I have been counted worthy to be Your faithful champions in this struggle against Satan just as Job was in the Old Testament. No matter what happens, we are sure of Your love for us and we remain loyal to You Lord. We are not ashamed to call You our God and to proclaim Jesus as Lord. We are saved and redeemed - VICTORIOUS in Christ Jesus. We are more than conquerors through Christ Jesus who strengthens us.

Please help us to remain faithful and loyal to You.

February 11, 2009
Subject: Good, Good and Better News

Hi Everyone,

Well the absolutely impossible and against all odds has happened again. Larry was able to eat four ounces of baby food both on Thursday and Friday for the Speech Therapist without a single hitch, and that after not having anything by mouth since December 26th. No one could have expected such a fabulous performance even if he had been practicing during the last month. So the Speech Therapist ordered a modified Barium Swallow on Monday, during which Larry gobbled up every consistency of food without any challenge whatsoever. Yesterday, Larry was able to eat pureed sausage, pancakes and thickened milk and orange juice. Starting on Monday, he will start eating two meals each day. We now have very realistic expectations for removing the feeding tube within the next 30 days! Praise God!

Now, as if that was not enough good news, tomorrow Larry will be transferred from the hospital wing to the skilled nursing level of the building, and his roommate will be the same man that protected him like a mother hen in the hospital wing. God is so good. Larry is qualified to receive 64 more days of care at this level, so he should be coming home again in April.

This sudden and rapid transformation has far exceeded all the expectations of his Doctor and the staff. Praise be to God!

Joyfully His,
Larry & Stacie

February 12, 2007
Subject: Journal Entry

I desire to maintain a white hot relationship with You my Lord. Holy Spirit, fire up my spirit to pursue You the way I want to. If I have allowed our relationship to cool off Lord, please forgive me, and help me mend it.

February 13, 2009
Subject: Peace

Hi Everyone,

"Faith believes in spite of the circumstances and acts in spite of the consequences." ~ Adrain Rogers

"God gives everyone certain attributes, characteristics and talents, then He says, 'If you use what you have I'll increase it, but if you don't use it, you'll lose it.' Use it or lose it; it's a law." ~ Charlie "Tremendous" Jones

"In the middle of every difficulty comes opportunity." ~ Albert Einstein

A very curious thing happened today. I went to visit Larry in his new room with two children in tow while his roommate watched TV at full volume and the hectic hubbub of any skilled nursing facility in the background. The scene was tumultuous to say the least. I asked Larry's roommate if he would consider turning down the TV, and instead, he turned it completely off so that I could read our devotions to Larry without distraction. The two children became perfectly still and quiet. The din of noise in the hallway became silent except for the nurse at the doorway, who prepared medications while she listened as I read aloud from the Bible for about 30 minutes. It was so surreal, like envisioning "Silent Night."

"Do what you can, with what you have, where you are." ~ Theodore Roosevelt

Larry and I pray that each of you will use this Presidents' Day Holiday and Valentines' weekend to assess how you can share the love of God with others in your sphere of influence.

Joyfully His,
Larry & Stacie

February 16, 2009
Subject: We love you!

Hi Everybody,

We thought that many of you would enjoy this very poignant article from Dr. Charles Stanley.

Our Choices in the Midst of Tragedy
Job (pronounced: Jobe) 1:6-2:8
By Dr. Charles Stanley

Imagine for a moment what it must have felt like to be in Job's sandals. Warriors, fire, and wind wiped out his vast fortune and killed his children. To add injury to insult, his boil-infested body was so irritated that he scratched at the inflamed skin with a shard of pottery. Had Job believed in luck rather than the Lord's sovereignty, He likely would have taken his wife's advice to "curse God and die" (2:9).

Job was brought low and he didn't know why. Read the book carefully, and you'll notice that he never learned the reason behind his testing. The reader is privy to the conversation between God and Satan, but the Lord did not share those details with his humbled servant. Left in the dark, Job had to decide if his faith in God's goodness would stand. Viewing the new chapter in his life as part of the Lord's larger plan (42:2), Job made a courageous choice to trust God in the midst of tragedy. The impoverished man could have railed against God, as his wife suggested. Or he might have followed his friends' unwise advice and racked his brain for an unconfessed sin that earned divine punishment. But neither of those actions would have been fruitful. Instead, Job acknowledged God's right to do to him whatever He desired for the glory of His name (Job 1:21).

Accepting the good things that God sends our way is easy. Our challenge is to receive tragedy with a willing attitude and a teachable spirit. Chance is not part of the equation—nothing comes into our life except through the Lord's permission (end of article).

We have seen many of our friends going through great tribulation in their lives, and it is so valuable to remember that this life is just a fleeting breath. Keep the perspective that God loves you and has your good in mind regardless of your temporary circumstances.

Nowhere in God's Word does He promise that life will be easy, but He does promise it will all be WORTH IT.

No eye has seen, no ear has heard, no mind has conceived what God has prepared for those who love Him. 1 Corinthians 2: 9

Because of what we have been through; Larry and I are especially sensitive to encouraging each of you to grow and to stand firm in your faith that Our God loves us and is working everything out for the good of those who BELIEVE!

Joyfully His,

Larry & Stacie

February 17, 2009
Subject: Journal Entry

Lord, thank you for the courage to live my life totally to suit You and not conform to what the world may think. I do not want to live an average life. I want to serve You outrageously Lord!

February 26, 2009
Subject: Journal Entry

God, You use events, people and the promptings of the Holy Spirit to move me into the center of Your will. I may not like the task You have assigned me, but I know You want it done, so it must be worthwhile.

Surely St. Paul did not want to be shipwrecked, beaten or imprisoned but You allowed all of these events in his life and he hung on to the tassels of Your robe all the harder.

When all hope is gone, I have hope. I have Your word, Your promises, Your vision of Larry restored and our vow to You to bring millions home with us for the wedding supper!

March 13, 2009
Subject: Journal Entry

Lord it seems that Larry is imprisoned by his body, which will not allow him to communicate or walk. Joseph was imprisoned and he stayed faithful to You. He stayed focused on the dream You gave him just as Larry does now.

Chapter 5

ॐॐ

March 19, 2009
Subject: Update

Hello Everyone,

We have endured some challenges since I last wrote, and I just couldn't find words worth writing, so I didn't. But not to worry, Larry is fine and will be coming home on April 17th. This date is being driven by insurance, not by his health status.

We have learned that God's call for each person is unique. He will provide the words, ability and circumstances so that you can achieve what He wants done. Remember, our Father is the one who makes the difference. We are merely tools, and we're blessed to be used by Him.

Anything worth having requires work! *Endure hardness, as a good soldier of Jesus Christ.* (2 Timothy 2:3). We know that your personal time and effort to pray for us requires work, and we are grateful for your ardent faith in God for Larry's complete restoration.

We love each and every one of you, and thank God for you every day. We pray that through your hectic lives and challenges that you stay your thoughts on your Redeemer, Protector, Savior and the best friend that you could ever imagine, Jesus.

Joyfully His,
Larry & Stacie

March 29, 2009
Subject: More Challenges

Hi Everyone,

A lot has happened since I last wrote. We have endured some very significant and weird challenges that are certainly last ditch efforts to get us to take our eyes off of Jesus and be overwhelmed. It's a good thing that we walk by faith and not by sight! Remember that it is always darkest just before the dawn and following every storm is God's rainbow! Larry formed words today for the first time since November and mimicked my words to him. I was so excited until I realized just how much that I had taken God's miracles for granted just like the Israelites did. I mean here I was acting like this was the first amazing sign that God had ever given me. In fact, the reality is that Larry was declared leukemia free 18 months ago, then died and was spectacularly brought back to life 17 months ago. Each day that Larry has lived since his resurrection defies all odds to the point of being a statistical impossibility. Why do we have a tendency to forget the good stuff while remembering the bad stuff?

Larry is coming home on the 17th of April and I am feverishly preparing. Many people have looked at me with long sympathetic stares and shook their heads wondering how I do for Larry what it take three shifts of well-trained professionals do 24/7. Well, here are some thoughts for your hearts to meditate on and to digest:

"Being deeply loved by someone gives you strength; loving someone deeply gives you courage." ~ Lao Tzu

"Plenty of people miss their share of happiness, not because they never found it, but because they didn't stop to enjoy it."
~ William Feather

The joy of the Lord is your strength. (Nehemiah 8:10)

> I am an immortal being headed for Heaven instead of Hell. I can do all things through Christ Jesus who strengthens me. Happiness is contagious....Be a carrier!

Joyfully His,
Larry & Stacie

April 4, 2009
Subject: Journal Entry

> Remember who I am and Whose I am!!!!!
> I have been in a life and death struggle for Larry since July 2007. Like Moses fought off vultures from his sacrifice, so I have been fighting demons trying to take Larry before his sacrifice is complete!
> Yes Lord, not that I am anyone important, but Christ dwelling in me makes me righteous.
> The joy of the Lord is my strength. I trust in You Lord. You are my rock and my salvation. In You alone I trust; not in men, governments and certainly not in me. Thank You Lord for giving me such a peace, security and joy in my almighty God! My God is big enough! My God is bigger than any human mind can comprehend! My God is totally willing and able to meet all my needs and righteous desires through Christ Jesus His only begotten Son. All glory, honor, praise and worship belong to You my God! You alone are worthy! Rejoice always!

April 6, 2009
Subject: Challenges and Rewards

Hello Everyone,

This past week was extremely challenging for us, but it was also very rewarding in that we have been completely renewed in our faith that our God is certainly in control and is working everything out for our good and for those around us.

On both Wednesday and Thursday we went by ambulance to a hospital for some very high-tech nuclear medicine procedures. Then on Friday, we went to a special hospital to receive two pints of blood. Over a three-day period, Larry spent about 27 hours on gurneys, which was harsh on him and detrimental to his bed sores. While we were gone on Friday, Larry's doctor ordered that he be moved to an isolation room upon his return because his immune system is suppressed. He also lost more weight and is down to 138 lbs.

I am sure you are asking yourself just how any of this can be an example of God's goodness or control?

First of all, please do not underestimate for a minute that God is the only excuse for Larry's continued survival everyday! Every medical person who sees him is slapped directly in the face with the same burning question: "What in the world is keeping this guy alive?" It is when they ask what happened that I am able to share his testimony and God with them. We have directly impacted the lives of 30 people this week, as well as six ambulance crews to include praying with two of them for God's protection and wisdom in their lives.

Larry's courage to continue living in order to serve God no matter how demeaning or in any capacity is why he is my hero. His quality of life is horrific, and yet he made a promise to God to do ANYTHING that God needed of him. Our God extracts the greatest amount of good out of the most vile of circumstances. Because of Larry's faithful perseverance to continue living, God has been brought into the forefront of at least a thousand minds that we know of in some capacity. There is a weird rhetorical question in the Bible that asks, "When Jesus returns will he still find faith?" I pray that through Larry's sacrifice that your faith in God is inspired.

Joyfully His,
Larry & Stacie

April 13, 2009
Subject: Journal Entry

Lord, You know how much I wanted to return to Africa in February and now again in April. Thank You for showing me that part of my motivation may not be for noble reasons. I crave travel and adventure, but I need to be still and be sure I do all things for Your honor and glory and not my own. Please forgive me Lord. I love You.

April 14, 2009
Subject: A Bump in the Road

Hello Everyone,

Last week Larry received another pint of blood and then the following day spiked his highest temperature yet. He is receiving a new antibiotic and only ibuprofen for pain, because the other choices are affecting his liver and kidneys. He is still in a private isolation room for his protection, so if you go to visit him be prepared to put on a gown, gloves and a mask.

Wednesday night, while in a class at church, I had an amazing encounter with a man who is actually deacon. His comments would have caused a less mature person to never return to church again! I was totally appalled at his lack of sensitivity and hardness toward me especially since he had never met me before this class. The worst part is that he would never have intentionally hurt anyone's feelings but fell victim to using Christian clichés' without engaging his heart or mind.

Neither my brother nor my son attend church anymore as a result of people who were much more interested in espousing how much they knew rather than how much they cared. I got to thinking why do we even go to church here? The answer is that this is the particular church that God specifically called Larry and I to. Neither of us had ever stepped a foot inside a church of this denomination before just because of their reputation as critics!

This event reminded me of how many of you do not attend church on a regular basis and I started wondering why? Maybe it is because we don't expect someone who is a church-goer to be a totally insensitive idiot! But then is any grouping of people immune from idiots? Isn't there always a percentage of whackos in every sector of the population? So what is the big deal about even going to church at all? Since Christianity is the only religion that practices a personal relationship with God through Jesus, what do I need all of these other people for, let alone buildings?

Buildings simply make it easier for us to come together in the unity of the Holy Spirit to worship our worthy God. Just as a team can accomplish far more than an individual, so a group of faith-filled believers can move Heaven and Earth with their prayers. How is a team rendered ineffective? By succumbing to offense, division and strife between the members. It is the enemy that desires to steal, kill and destroy the body of Christ by causing strife, division and offense within the members. The enemy can easily use that small percentage of self-focused idiots to rip apart the best of teams, so how much more vulnerable are those believers who refuse to associate with the team for love, encouragement and protection in prayer?

The church team that I choose to associate with will never be perfect as long as it is comprised of human beings, but in God's divine tapestry my membership in it will exponentially bless Him.

The effective fervent prayer of a righteous person avails much. Larry and I continue to pray for the unity of the body of Christ, and we hope that this e-mail has touched your heart to be a contributing part of the team, warts and all, and not part of the other skill set.

Joyfully His,
Larry & Stacie

April 21, 2009
Subject: Journal Entry

Lord God in the name of Your Son Jesus we need to see the manifestation of Your love and power in this world.

God, You are our awesome Father and You desire to bless Your children and give them the desires of their hearts. You are the One True and Living God, I know it is Your desire to have a free flowing relationship with mankind. Lord let us see the manifestation of Your power in response to our prayers.

We pray for Your miraculous power to once again be displayed in Larry, as well as everyone else that we have prayed with and for. God, please allow Larry and I to take Your power to the world. We thank You for this precious time of preparation for the worldwide ministry that You have destined for us. We are not asking for Your miraculous restoration for our own comfort or reward, but for the purpose of sharing Your power and love into a world ripe for resurrection. Resurrect Mankind!

April 22, 2009
Subject: Be Part of a Miracle

Hello Everyone,

Larry and I spent Friday getting an MRI done on his pelvic region and left foot to make sure that he does not have a bone infection in either of those locations as a result of stage four bed sores. He remains in isolation as a result of a low white blood cell count.

Late Friday night and Tuesday, Larry received yet another pint of whole blood and is getting a bunch of antibiotics for numerous things, but mostly for pneumonia that he has contracted despite all of our precautions. Today the doctor confirmed that Larry has an infection in the bones along his spinal column. As a result, he was implanted with a PIC-line today so that he can receive six weeks of intensive antibiotic therapy. (A PIC-line is an IV port for long-term medication infusion and carries everything directly into the heart.)

To be blatantly honest, Larry needs a miracle, and he needs it now. I don't think that there are any atheists on this list, so I am going to speak to you all as believers. What do all believers have in common? Prayer. Even if that prayer is only one word in length, God hears you, always. Nothing is impossible for God the Creator of all things both seen and unseen. If God is for us, who can be against us? Or better yet, if God is for us, what difference does it make who is against us?

I am issuing a blanket invitation for each one of you as believers to pray the prayer of faith for Larry's sevenfold restoration for all that Satan has come to steal, kill and destroy in him. It blesses God tremendously when His children actually believe that what He has promised in His word is true, and that He is well able to perform that which He has promised.

Assuredly, I (Jesus) say to you, whatever you bind on earth will be bound in heaven, and whatever you loose on earth will be loosed in heaven. For where two or three are gathered together in My name, I am there in the midst of them. (Matthew 18:18-20)

So Jesus answered and said to them, "Assuredly, I say to you, if you have faith and do not doubt, you will not only do what was done to the fig tree, but also if you say to this mountain, 'Be removed and be cast into the sea,' it will be done. And whatever things you ask in prayer, believing, you will receive." (Matthew 21:21-22)
So Jesus answered and said to them, 'Have faith in God, for assuredly, I say to you, whoever says to this mountain, 'Be removed and cast into the sea,' and does not doubt in his heart, but believes that those things he says will be done, he will have whatever he says. Therefore I say to you, whatever things you ask for when you pray, believe that you receive them, and you will have them. (Mark 11:22-24)

And He (Jesus) said to them, "Go into the world and preach the good news to every creature. He who believes and is baptized will be saved; but he who does not believe will be condemned. And these signs will follow those who believe: in my name they will cast out demons; they will speak with new tongues; they will take up serpents; and if they drink anything deadly, it will by no means hurt them; they will lay hands on the sick, and they will recover." (Mark 16:15-18)

"I (Jesus) have come that they may have life, and that they may have it more abundantly." (John 10:10)

Jesus Christ is the same yesterday, today and forever. (Hebrews 13:8)

Is anyone among you sick? Let him call for the elders of the church, and let them pray over him, anointing him with oil in the name of the Lord. And the prayer of faith will save the sick, and the Lord will raise him up. And if he has committed sins, they will be forgiven. Confess your trespasses to one another, that you may be healed. The effective, fervent prayer of the righteous man avails much. (James 5:14-16)

Now this is the confidence that we have in Him, that if we ask anything according to His will, He hears us. And if we know that He hears us, whatever we ask, we know that we have the petitions that we have asked of Him. (1 John 5:14-15)

We are all going to die sometime and Larry has had at least 15 major miracles in the last 21 months so why am I still asking for the whole enchilada? Because just like Lazarus, Larry still has a mission to accomplish. His restoration is not so that he can live out the rest of his days in comfort and ease. To quote Larry and Psalm 118:17, *"I shall not die, but live, and declare the works of the Lord."* The purpose for Larry's restoration is for us to fulfill our destiny in Christ Jesus.

Thank you once again for your prayers filled with ardent faith and belief.

Joyfully His,
Larry & Stacie

April 23, 2009
Subject: Journal Entry

Lord of all the life events I have remembered, I now see how You have prepared Larry and I (the most unlikely of people) to fulfill the great commission through our lives. Larry lives to proclaim Your works, Your deeds, Your goodness to all of mankind. Our destiny is to be living examples of Your goodness and faithfulness and to tell everyone whom we come into contact with! Lord, I look forward in joy to the day Larry and I are counted worthy to die because of our testimony for Your Son Christ Jesus. I see everything that we are enduring now as preparation for our ultimate destiny as a result of leading millions to You through Yeshua Messiah. We love and praise You and worship You with all of our ability! God, You are so good. Thank You for choosing us. Thank You for trusting us Lord!

"The Spirit of the Lord has come upon me, because He has anointed me to preach the good news to the poor. To heal the broken hearted. To preach deliverance to the captives and the recovery of the sight to the blind. To set at liberty the bruised. To preach the acceptable year of the Lord." ~ Jesus

April 29, 2009
Subject: 18 Months Ago

Hello Everyone,

Today marks 18 months since Larry died and was miraculously resurrected by the power and authority in the name of Jesus Christ.

A few weeks ago I told you about a man at church that said some inappropriate things about our situation. The next week he apologized very sincerely to me in front of the entire class. He felt so bad because he would never intentionally hurt anyone. I realized that I am also very zealous for the Lord, and tact has never been a strong suit for me either, but I am working on it.

Please except my heartfelt apology for hurting any one of you by remarks that I have made in the past. As a matter of fact, please let me know, not if, but how I have injured you so that I can specifically and personally make amends.

Joyfully His,
Stacie

May 10, 2009
Subject: A Phenomenal Day

Hello Our Dear Family,

This afternoon while reading aloud to Larry, as I do daily, I was aware that someone had entered the room, but remained perfectly still while I finished reading Psalm 136. Being as it was Mother's Day and Larry's mother is in Heaven, it really touched my heart. I couldn't help but to cry at both the beauty and the irony of it.

It was shocking to see that the silent person in the room was Larry's nurse (who looked like T.D. Jakes' younger brother), and he proceeded to give me a breath stifling bear hug and skillfully prayed for the both of us. I am not talking about some limp-wristed, lukewarm, sissy prayer, but of one who truly knows God. It was so amazing as we continued to praise God while he hung bags of antibiotics and food over my sweet husband in thanksgiving for God's mercy and miraculous healing. It was spectacular!

Larry's condition continues to be problematic, but he has stabilized, and he seems happy and peaceful.

"Trusting God completely means having faith that He knows what is best for your life. You expect Him to keep His promises, help you with problems, and do THE IMPOSSIBLE when necessary." - Rick Warren "The Purpose Driven Life"

Joyfully His,
Larry & Stacie

May 18, 2009
Subject: Preparation

Hello Everyone,

We love and pray blessings on each and every one of you. What an amazing journey that the Lord has called all of us to travel. We thank God continually for your love and friendship.

Larry continues to hold stable even though he is still in isolation for his own protection. There is amazing joy and peace in his eyes and there are no words to describe the godly presence in his room. Even when I am afraid or discouraged I leave his room refreshed.

The Lord reminds us that most of the problems that we encounter are of our own design. But God has specifically allowed a few tailored events to test and to grow our character. Many of you may be facing situations that are not of your doing and that are completely out of your control to change or correct. Do you know how to respond in a crisis, whether it is spiritual, emotional, physical, social or financial? Do you know what to do in order to endure under a sustained attack?

We have just entered hurricane season here and so we are checking our lists for supplies and evacuation routes to make sure that we safeguard life and property to the best of our ability. But when all is said and done; to what or to whom is your life-line tied? Larry and I can assure you that God will never give you a bigger storm than He is willing to carry you through. Be wise and take every precaution to control your environment, but recognize opportunities to grow closer to God in your helplessness.

Joyfully His,
Larry & Stacie

June 4, 2009
Subject: Happy Birthday Larry

Hi Everyone,

Yes today Larry turned 68. What an outstanding miracle that is. There is simply no excuse outside of God for Larry to have even survived these last 22 months! It is fabulously astounding.

Larry was born at home and his Aunt "B" gave him his cute little belly button. He is the baby in a family of seven children. So there you have your little known Larry facts.

Now for some birthday wisdom: "The only people you should try to get even with are those who have helped you. And when you set out for revenge, be sure to dig two graves." ~ Larry Ebinger (Larry's brother from another Mother, because they think so much alike)

Joyfully His,
Larry & Stacie

June 13, 2009

Subject: Living on the Edge

Hi Everyone,

We have had quite a roller coaster ride this week, but I have gotten so used to it that I no longer scream, kick, cry or vomit. Yes it is true that we can become accustomed to bombs going off all around us, but the trick is not to let your heart grow calloused or expect the circumstances to remain so excruciating forever, thus losing hope. We may not know when it will end or how it will end, but we can be certain that it will end one way or another.

I had no sooner finished a long and complicated meeting with the head of social services yesterday about Larry's discharge from the hospital to a skilled nursing facility when I went upstairs and his doctor informed me that as a result of receiving the latest test reports that everything had instantly changed every plan we had just ironed out. Living on the edge of life minute to minute and day by day and month in and month out can be an excruciating experience.

During the exciting but challenging times in which we live, the devil is maximizing one of his favorite tools; the big D word—discouragement. When faced with the big D it is very easy to give up, become depressed and wallow in a sewer of plague-infested self-pity.

"It's never as bad as it seems in that moment. Remember to have a good perspective and know that good days are still ahead of you no matter what you may be feeling right now. The Lord Jesus reminds us to have a proper perspective and know that the latter joys will greatly overshadow the former miseries that came our way as read in John 16:21-22, '*A woman, when she is in labor, has sorrow because her hour has come; but as soon as she has given birth to the child, she no longer remembers the anguish, for joy that a human being has been born into the world. Therefore you now have sorrow; but I will see you again and your heart will rejoice, and your joy no one will take from you.'* " ~ Dwayne Savaya

The Lord promises to replace every trial and tribulation that we go through with joy unspeakable so be encouraged and know that weeping may endure for a night, but joy comes in the morning. (1 Peter 1:6-9) (Psalm 30:5)

Now we are children - heirs of God and co-heirs with Christ, if indeed we share in His sufferings in order that we may also share in His glory. I consider that our present sufferings are not worth comparing to the glory that will be revealed in us. (Romans 8:17-18)

The devil wages war against all of mankind. However, as believers, there is no excuse for not believing that the Lord is not only able but earnestly desires to fulfill ALL of His promises. It is impossible to please God without faith, so be encouraged and fear not!

Joyfully His,
Larry & Stacie

June 22, 2009
Subject: Still in Isolation

Hello Everyone,

Larry still remains in a private isolation room at the hospital level of care. We have gone through numerous iterations of infections and ensuing changes in his antibiotic regime. One thing has become painfully clear to me and that is that my part is to protect him in prayer and not become so involved in the crisis that each moment might bring. Healthy visitors are always welcome, but you must be willing to deal with the inconvenience of dressing up in some very unfashionable apparel.

I am in the process of creating another collage of pictures so that Larry and I can get back to the business of interceding for all of you. If necessary, just line up against a wall and have a friend take a head shot of your family and get it to me in the next two weeks. We promise that it will be a blessing to us as much as it is to you.

"Perseverance is not a long race: it is many short races, one after another." ~Walter Elliot

Perseverance, gentleness and patience do not come easily to me. I have to work at developing these traits in my character but they have served me well in being able to endure hardship. Many of you are suffering through a painful event and have a need to develop some characteristic which will help carry you through the valley.

A long time ago someone said to me, "If you don't put God first in your day then He is not first in your life." That statement has had a profound affect on my life. It was stupendously hypocritical to call myself a Christian and not read the owner's manual. As a baby Christian I didn't have a clue about how to talk to God for any more than a 15 second plea for help every so often. Then I discovered that God would talk with me if I would just read His word. I didn't need to have the Ten Commandments memorized, or know any religious rules for God to be willing to personally teach me right out of His "Textbook for the Human Being."

I promise you that if you will just start with 10 minutes every day, it will revolutionize your life and you'll be amazed at what God will do through you when you give God's Word priority. But let me warn you, don't wait until you think you have the time. Satan will see to it that you never do. Remember that you are more than a conqueror in Christ Jesus and nothing is impossible for God.

Joyfully His,
Larry & Stacie

July 4, 2009
Subject: Why ask why?

Hello Everyone,

On Thursday Larry moved from the third floor to the second floor of the hospital. He is still in a private room, and he has become more stable in that he has not had a blood transfusion for three weeks now!

This has been a long arduous journey and sometimes I get a little weary and forget all that I have to be grateful for. I have to jerk myself out of that bad place in my thoughts. The Lord asked me to share the following journal entry with all of you.....

What difference does it make why God allows awful things to happen? Does questioning God change the situation? Who am I that God would have to justify Himself to me? Would knowing why somehow justify my 4-year-old nephew dying from a bullet in his brain? Larry's leukemia diagnosis, remission and then heart failure? Would knowing why make any situation in my life less painful? NO! So why further jeopardize my soul by playing right into Satan's hand by questioning and even accusing God of doing wrong for allowing all of these hideous things that have happened in my life? Why not ask God the productive questions like: What do You want me to do or how do You want me to act in this situation Lord? How can I overcome the evil in this situation with good Lord? Lord, please heal my broken heart. Lord, please help me to forgive and supernaturally forget just like You do with our sins. Please Lord help me get over, under, around or through any obstacle the devil has put in my path to distract me from accomplishing the ultimate goal You have designed for my life. (End of journal entry)

Each of you were created with a specific destiny in God's mind. When you seek to know your Father, He has promised to reveal His purpose for your existence. Jesus never promised us a rose garden, on the contrary, He promised that we would SUFFER and be PERSECUTED for His Name's sake. Let's pull up our panties and act like the mighty warriors that our God has called us to be. Let's saddle up and put on the full armor of God and strike into battle with our real enemy in the spiritual realm! No more self-focused pity parties, poor me or victim mentality! We are overcomers! We are the righteousness of God! We are more than conquerors in Christ Jesus! Nothing is impossible with God! Without a battle there can be no victory! Take up your cross and wage war! The victory was won for us on a cross 2,000 years ago!

Joyfully His,
Larry & Stacie

July 12, 2009
Subject: Joy

Hi Everybody,

Two years ago today Larry and I received the news that he had leukemia. With all that has happened, it seems like 20 years ago now.

144

Larry is still in the hospital but is getting stronger every day. His morale is much higher than it has been in a long time as well. It is possible that Larry will be coming home on Thursday July 16th but there are a number of factors that could alter this date by as much as 14 days.

We have discovered that there is not enough trauma, poison or disease to kill a man and not enough medicine to keep him alive. God alone cured Larry of cancer, resurrected him from the dead and now continues to sustain his life in the face of all medical science.

The joy of the Lord is your strength. (Nehemiah 8:10)

"Plenty of people miss their share of happiness, not because they never found it, but because they didn't stop to enjoy it."
~ William Feather

"Although the world is full of suffering, it is also full of the overcoming of it."~ Helen Keller

"You can be greater than anything that can happen to you."
~ Norman Vincent Peale

Joy is a very real force, and the devil doesn't have anything that can stand up against it. Just as fear has to yield to faith, discouragement has to yield to joy. Since joy is one of the fruits of the Spirit, (every born again spirit) you already have it residing within you. But you must develop it, confess it and live by it if you want to harness its power. Whatever circumstances you are facing today, you can be full of joy. You can be strong in the Lord. You can draw on the supply of the Holy Spirit within you and come out on top.

Joyfully His,
Larry & Stacie

Chapter 6

❧❦

August 9, 2009
Subject: Larry is Home

Hi Everybody,

Larry came home on Friday July 17. Sorry for the delay
in writing, but I have been getting back into the groove
and working hard at getting Larry adjusted to new sched-
ules in treatment and drug administration. He is obviously
very happy to be home, and he seems to be getting healthier
everyday.

It's such an astounding miracle that Larry has made yet
another comeback and been able to return home. His last
illness can only testify to the fact that God is amazingly merciful and still doing the impossible. Any day in the past eight
months could have been Larry's last and there is simply
no medical explanation for how he survived the last three
months! (They have been terrifyingly awful)

Larry's new doctor came to the house and was totally
amazed at his mental acuity and responses to me. The doctor
was so astonished that you could see his jaw drop as he
looked at Larry's diagnosis and then back at us with a perplexed look. It is always interesting to watch people's reac-
tions as I recount what exactly happened that left Larry in

this condition, because it is so clear that it is only by divine intervention that Larry is still with us everyday for nearly two years!

I want each of you to close your eyes and visualize yourself as clay and God as the master pot maker. Although some clay does not lend itself to being manipulated, you have chosen to be pliable and submissive to the process. First there is the squishing and squeezing and mushing and mashing to get a uniform consistency. Then comes the punching and pounding to remove any air pockets that would cause you to explode later. Now you are being rolled up in a ball and abruptly slapped onto the spinning wheel where you are spun endlessly and gently shaped into a tall cylindrical vase. Finally, you stop spinning but you are still frightfully dizzy and ready to vomit, then you sit on a shelf for a long time with no contact, seemingly forgotten.

About a year later the potter takes you off of the shelf and starts to rub you with abrasive cloth to smooth off your roughness and wrinkles. Then He coats you in a penetrating acid solution that stings like crazy which opens up all of your pores and makes you vulnerable and permeable to paint, but now you are stuck on a shelf for at least three long days in excruciating pain. Next comes a beautiful thick warm white glaze that thoroughly coats you inside and out and you are allowed to rest and soak in this purity for 24 hours until you face the first in the most hideous challenges you will ever encounter; being fired in a horrifically hot kiln for the next 24 hours. Having survived the kiln you are grateful for the opportunity to rest on the shelf for however long the Potter wants to leave you there. Just when you are content to be left alone, you are snatched up and scorched by the soot of a candle to make erratic black marks all over your exterior then gently sprayed with a clear glaze and once again abruptly tossed back into that awful furnace. Then just when you are thinking that you have survived and that the ordeal is finally over and you have grown cold, the master's hand grips you and starts carving intricate designs into you, there is no escape! Oh, no, what now? Molten lava is being poured into these open wounds but at this point you are thinking that at least they will be seared and filled so that you will not become too weakened, fragile or susceptible to breakage. And of course, finally you are sprayed with another clear glaze and thrown back into the hell hole! When you emerge, you discover that the potter has designed you to be a very precious and rare type of water pitcher resembling marbled granite inlayed with spectacularly precious metals, fit for the use of the a king.

So the point of my parable is if you are sure that your loving heavenly Father will never do anything to harm you and actually only has your best interest in His heart, then perhaps you can endure any hardship. If I had told you in the beginning what a spectacular vessel the Lord was creating with you then you would have rationalized that whatever you had to go through would have been worth it to achieve your beautiful divine destiny. Well here is the truth ... God has a glorious plan for your life, but to succeed you must exercise your faith and that requires extreme effort sometimes. So now you have no excuse for saying, "Why God do I have to go through all of these challenges in my life?" Just stay focused on Jesus, the ultimate living water pitcher.

Joyfully His,
Larry & Stacie

August 14, 2009
Subject: Ooooooops!

Hello Everyone,

My Larry spiked a high temperate on Monday afternoon and his vital signs were not pretty, so the home health nurses called the ambulance to have Larry whisked off to the ER where he was admitted in order to receive massive IV antibiotics.

I am expecting Larry to be released home next week with continued IV therapy.

Also on Monday about 20 youth from our church came to put a new roof on our house, and they were able to finish way ahead of schedule just in time for the continuation of "Monsoon Summer" here in Virginia. We have been so blessed and encouraged by all of the love and support lavished upon us during our ordeal. What makes it even better is that none of these things have been done for us out of pity or obligation but out of love just as it was exemplified between the believers in the book of Acts. I am so glad to live in such a time as this when the church is preparing for the soon return of Jesus. Jesus is returning for a church without spot or blemish. That means that His people (the body of Christ) will be perfected in unselfish love and washed pure by His precious blood.

Patience is a steadfastness of soul; the quality that does not surrender to circumstances. Let patience have her perfect work in your life.

Joyfully His,
Larry & Stacie
August 20, 2009
Subject: More Surgery for Larry

Hi Everyone,

Larry is still in the hospital although he probably could have come home yesterday. Based upon the recommendations of some physicians and after prayerful consideration,

Larry will have surgery tomorrow to install a colostomy. It probably would have been better if it had been done a long time ago. I am at complete peace and agreement with this.

Please pray for the surgical staff and specifically for the salvation of his surgeon. Remember that nothing is by coincidence but only by Godincidence! I am continually blessed by how God maneuvers us to impact lives for His Kingdom. The Lord continues to add to the number of witnesses daily that will attest that Larry's healing could have only been accomplished by God Himself and that no man could possibly take credit for it.

Joy has nothing to do with circumstances; it is a decision. The joy of the Lord is truly our strength so plant the vision of everlasting joy in God's Kingdom in your mind's eye, and then go infect your world. I promise that you will experience 30, 60 or 100 times the amount of joy that you sow in love to those whom you come into contact.

The following scriptures are some suggested reading for you to think about in order to develop the fruit of joy in your heart: Matthew 25:21, Luke 2:10, Luke 15:7-10, John 15:11, John 16:20-24.

Joyfully His,
Larry & Stacie

August 21, 2009
Subject: Flying colors

Hello Everyone,

Larry's surgery went even smoother than expected. Although I have no clue as to how soon he will be home, I am planning on Monday.

Before surgery we had quite a bit of private time to pray and talk together about God's will and destiny for our lives. As crazy as this may sound, we have been blessed to have God's and our priorities so intricately aligned.

We were avid God seekers before Larry got sick, but since then we were instantly propelled into formulating a "Bucket List." You know the one where you write down everything that you wanted to do or accomplish with your life? We asked God to show us what our "Life Song" was to be as a tribute to Him before one of us left this planet.

We have discovered that many tunes comprise a song, and many songs comprise a symphony, which can be analogized as the summation of one's life.

One of the songs that Larry and I started singing in July of 2007 is found in 2 Corinthians 4:16-5:1; *Therefore we do not lose heart. Even though our outward man is perishing, yet the inward man is being renewed day by day. For our light affliction, which is but for a moment, is working for us a far more exceeding and eternal weight of glory; while we look not at the things which are seen, but at the things which are not seen: for the things which are seen are temporary; but the things which are not seen are eternal. For we know that if our earthly house, this tent, is destroyed, we have a building from God, a house not made with hands, eternal in the heavens.*

Because your circumstances may not be as harsh as ours this might put you at a disadvantage, because you may think that you have all the time in the world. As a personal favor to Larry and I, we are asking each of you to set aside a little time this week to make a bucket list and to ask God to reveal His symphony for your life. Here is a clue: If there is something that really makes you happy or that you are really passionate about, then God has already predisposed or hardwired you to sing that song.

Please, next week we would love you to e-mail us and share your quest with us so that we can intercede and cover you in prayer.

Joyfully His,
Larry & Stacie

September 10, 2009
Subject: Matthew

Hello Everyone,

Our son, Matthew, went to Heaven at about 5 a.m. this morning. Please do not call me. I will provide more later.

Still joyfully His,
Stacie

Sept. 11, 2009
Subject: Unrighteous Anger by Dr. Stanley

Anger can shut down communication and break relationships apart. If suppressed, this emotion turns into resentment, which poisons thinking and behavior. Unchecked, it can boil over into an explosive expression of rage that hurts not only the intended recipient but others as well.

While we can think of many reasons to justify our anger, the only viewpoint that matters is the Lord's. From the book of Proverbs, we can gain insight into how God views angry people. He says they act foolishly (14:17), stir up strife (15:18), and commit transgressions (29:22). He also warns us not to associate with such individuals (22:24). In contrast, those who are slow to anger have great understanding

(14:29) and demonstrate wisdom (29:8, 11). Keeping one's distance from strife also shows honor (20:3).

In the New Testament, (James 1:19-20) the apostle James compared the tongue to a small spark that can set a whole forest on fire. (James 3:5-6) He knew the damage a furious person could do. He also wrote that our anger does not bring about the righteous life that God desires for us, nor does it fit who we are in Christ. Jesus paid our sin-debt with His life in order to set us free from sinful behavior.

The few times that Jesus became angry were fully in line with God's purposes. In us, however, that emotion is usually born of self-defense or thwarted desires. If God has convicted you of unrighteous anger, confess your sin and allow the Spirit to reproduce Christ's character in you.

For more biblical teaching and resources from Dr. Charles Stanley, please visit www.intouch.org

September 11, 2009
Subject: Funeral Arrangements

Hello Everyone,

A visiting nurse that did not know that I was not planning not to tell Larry about Matthews' death said something so I was forced to tell him. He cried. Then we both cried for a long time. Oh, God help us.

Matthews' funeral will be on Wednesday at our church at noon with burial to follow in the plot I thought I would be buried in.

We cannot thank you all enough for your outpouring of love and compassion.

Many blessings,
Larry & Stacie

September 12, 2009
Subject: What Happened?

Hello Everyone,

Because so many are asking and I just cannot tolerate to keep rehearsing this nightmare, please just let me say it in an e-mail.

Matthew was happily snoring one minute and not breathing the next. The toxicology report could take six weeks but it appears to be a prescription drug interaction. He had recently been prescribed a number of medications and a couple of them had death as a possible side effect.

We are trusting God to lead us through this tragedy and to extract the greatest amount of good in the lives of others through this experience.

We also rejoice in our sufferings, because we know that suffering produces perseverance; perseverance character and character hope. And hope does not disappoint us, because God has poured out his love into our hearts by the Holy Spirit, whom He has given us. (Romans 5:3)

Joyfully His,
Larry & Stacie

September 17, 2009
Subject: 7 Days Later

Hello Everyone,

Seven days ago I held my son's body and prayed as we waited for the coroner to arrive. Three days ago we buried Matthew's body. His body was merely his Earth suit, which allowed him to interact on this planet. The real Matthew, his spirit and soul, are in Heaven with Jesus now for all eternity.

I have asked God why. I have asked God to tell me what more He wants from me. What am I suppose to be doing here? The fact that Larry is still alive is just as shocking as Matthew's death! I am overwhelmed with agony and grief in both situations. Oh, God, I don't think I can take anymore!

God does not owe me an explanation. Everything I am I relinquish to my Creator and surrender to my Savior. I hold nothing back. I know that God loves Larry, Matthew and I more than we could ever imagine, and His will for us is only good whether I understand what happens or not.

The sacrifice of praise is my most precious weapon right now so I continue to sing of my love for the Lord for only He can heal any of our wounds.

Always joyfully His,
Stacie

September 28, 2009
Subject: Thank You

Hello Everyone,

"Courage does not always roar. Sometimes it is a quiet voice at the end of the day saying...I will try again tomorrow." ~ Mary Ann Radmacher

"Enjoy the little things, for one day you may look back and realize they were big things." ~ Robert Bault

Today I am thankful that God ever gave me a son at all. I am thankful for the courage to face another day. I am thankful that I listened to God and got out of the Army when

I did so that I had the opportunity to get to know my son, even though he was already nine years old. I am thankful that Larry was able to help raise him. I am thankful for the good Matthew was able to accomplish in the lives of others.

Please Lord use Matthew's death for some huge greater benefit in Your Kingdom. I am believing for You to use his death to change lives! Jesus let it be so!

God, You gave Your Son to die on a cross so that my son could die and live forever. Thank You.

Joyfully His,
Stacie

September 30, 2009
Subject: Ouch!

Hello Everyone,

Today included particularly hellish warfare. I had a major emotional meltdown, and I believe that I was probably hysterical a couple of times. I understand that this is all part of the grieving process, but I am also hoping that it will run its course more rapidly since I am not able to take any drugs so that I can care for Larry.

Larry spiked a very high temperature and his doctor said to take him to the ER. The ER was so busy that Larry was forced to lay on stretcher in the hallway the entire time before being admitted nine hours later.

Only God is keeping me sane at this point, because the agony I am experiencing is well beyond my threshold of endurance. It helps me to focus on what we have and how God has blessed us. I am thankful for magnificent family and friends that are constantly interceding in prayer on our behalf.

Create in me a pure heart, O God and renew a steadfast spirit within me. Do not cast me from Your presence or take Your Holy Spirit from me. Restore to me the joy of Your Salvation and grant me a willing spirit to sustain me. (Psalms 51:10-12)

Truly, we comprehend the gravity of what it means to offer up a sacrifice of praise and its value as a secret weapon in God's arsenal.

Joyfully His,
Larry & Stacie

October 4, 2009
Subject: Thoughts on Losing a Child

Hello Everyone,

Although Larry is still in the hospital he is much more animated than he was last week. He is on massive doses of IV antibiotics, and his fevers are under control as a result. I will find out the results of some critical blood tests tomorrow and perhaps a timeline for him to come home.

Shortly after being married in 1973 (my first marriage), we found out that we could not have children, which served as yet another nail in the coffin we loosely referred to as a marriage. By 1982 we were separated (literally, coast to coast) and filing for divorce when I discovered that I was pregnant. Because of these circumstances and the fact that I was a 2nd Lieutenant at the time, my Major counseled me to seriously consider having an abortion. That was the easy answer. I knew that there was no way for me to raise a child and be an Army Officer, so I quietly resolved to arrange for adoption rather than abortion. As it turned out God touched my husband's heart so that he wanted to reconcile and he took great care of us for a long time.

Before we were married, we agreed that a male child would be the fourth in namesake, but while looking at baby names we discovered that Matthew means, "Gift of the Lord," and so we instantaneously agreed to scratch tradition. This afternoon from 3 p.m. until 4 p.m. I stood in quiet prayer lined up on a busy street holding a sign stating, "Abortion Kills Children" as part of the "Life Chain" across America and Canada today. I sobbed for all of the women who lost their children to abortion, because they were too afraid or pressured or vulnerable to think they could give life to their babies. But, I specifically cried for those who were just self-focused at the time and now live in a hellish nightmare of "what ifs?"

I think that losing a child is the most gut wrenching experience that a person can know. Yet as a nation we have allowed God's sworn immortal enemy to deceive us into thinking that we are not actually killing little human beings. Jesus himself said that during the end-times the love of many would grow cold. I ask you to pray that the scales be removed from the eyes of our fellow Americans. After all, every child truly is a "Gift of the Lord."

Create in us a pure heart O God and renew our minds with Your unfailing love.

Joyfully His,
Larry & Stacie

October 7, 2009
Subject: Grief Counseling

Hello Everyone,

Larry is still in the hospital, and we are still awaiting the results of some blood tests. He is doing better as far as the fevers are concerned, but this is all very nerve wracking for everyone. Tomorrow afternoon, we should have all of the test results and I will be formulating a plan with his doctor.

A dear Kenyan brother recommended that I seek professional Christian grief counseling to help me grow through what has happened with Matthew, as well as Larry. I have already joined a program called Grief Share to guide me through 13 weeks of mourning. It has been invaluable to me in preparing for just what I can expect to experience emotionally. Each of us grieves differently, but there are some standard responses or gates that each of us need to pass through to achieve healing. I choose to advance through this process face first knowing that to do otherwise is to prolong the agony.

A lot of people in the last two years have told me that it is okay to be mad at God. But I just have no desire to be mad. Don't get me wrong, I have asked God what in the world He was thinking in allowing all of this happen to Larry, and now letting my only child die? Have I done something wrong? Am I being punished? What do You want me to do now? What do You expect from me God?

This was God's answer to me, "I expect your total faith, love, trust, devotion and unquestioning loyalty. I love you and only have your eternal good in mind. Lean on Me harder than ever before and expect Me to be your solid comfort. Do not allow yourself to be pulled off track by selfishness, pity parties, or the traditions and philosophy of mankind."

Although that was a pretty point blank response, at least I have a clear set of marching orders. The rest of the details are personal. This may sound a little crazy to a nonbeliever, but Christianity is about a personal relationship with our Creator. If you do not have two-way communication, what kind of relationship can you possibly have with anyone?

Joyfully His,
Larry & Stacie

October 14, 2009
Subject: 34 Days

Hello Everyone,

Well Thursday I had the big meeting with the doctor only to find out that the blood test results were inconclusive for what they were trying to determine. Also the doctor on the case had only met Larry two days prior. So Larry came home on Saturday and seems to be doing quite well. He looks great, and I was able to get him all spruced up with a hair cut so that he looks more Larry-like again.

Today marks 34 days since Matthew died. I cannot believe that it has been that long already. I am very grateful that my emotions have settled down a bit and that my decision to face this journey through the valley of death without artificial support from medication seems to be the best possible result for me. You see there is plenty of evidence that I have a genetic predisposition to be addicted. My paternal grandfather died drunk and destitute, my father had his challenges, but was delivered, a number of my siblings have had their struggles with alcohol, and Matthew and I attended a number of AA meetings together. The struggle to remain straight has been significant. I am grateful for the knowledge that my God is bigger than any temptation the devil can throw at me.

Please understand that I am NOT saying that it is wrong for people to use prescription drugs to alter their moods in times of extreme stress. It is just that I have found that in my particular circumstance and season of mourning that to take the straight line between two points while squeezing God's hand is the quickest and least painful approach of all the courses of action available. Sixty percent of all Americans are on some form of mood altering medication, and depression is the number one treated complaint in America. I recognize how vulnerable I am as well as my propensity to transfer dependence to substances, and so I just thank God for giving me His wisdom to trust in Him like a little child to get me through all of this.

We are in spiritual combat rather than physical therefore we dare not let our guard down.

Trust in the Lord with all your heart and lean not on your own understanding.

Joyfully His,
Larry & Stacie

October 25, 2009
Subject: Larry

Hello Everyone,

My dear husband, Larry, went home to be with Jesus at 2 a.m. this morning.

His funeral will be at our church in Virginia Beach. I do not have a date yet, but noon will allow the most people to attend. I will e-mail the date as soon as possible.

Larry will be buried in his Army Dress Blues with full military honors, and it would be a blessing to me if you could come in uniform.

We love you and thank you for all of your prayers.

Joyfully His,
Stacie

November 5, 2009
Subject: A New Day

Hello Everyone,

One week ago today we buried Larry. Godincidentally, we buried Larry the same day, hour and nearly the minute that he died in our kitchen two years ago. His home going service was beautiful and inspiring. The 21-gun salute and military ceremony at the grave side were a validation of Larry's selfless service to his country and to all who knew him.

Jesus raised Lazarus from the dead. Although Lazarus died again later, in the mean time his life served as an indisputable living monument to the love and power of God. Larry's life before as well as after his resurrection served the same purpose.

I am 54 years old and my son and husband are already in Heaven waiting for me. My only reason and purpose for continuing to live is to please my Creator. It is my heart's desire to forcefully pursue all that God has destined for me to accomplish in the time that I have left. (Lord, I relinquish all control to You! Your Holy Spirit controls my every action and thought)

"You find out who you are in your moments of greatest disappointment." ~ Robert Kiosaki

"Restore to me the joy of Your salvation, and uphold me by Your generous Spirit. Then I will teach transgressors Your ways and sinners shall be converted to You." (Psalm 51:12-13)

Joyfully His,
Stacie

November 11, 2009
Subject: The Journey Continues

Hello Everyone,

I want to thank all of you who have done so much for me and my family in the last two months. There is simply no way that I could have survived all of this sanely without your compassion and priceless prayers.

I believe that Larry died of a broken heart. He just couldn't find the strength to fight anymore after Matthew's death. He had already been to Heaven and he just couldn't force himself to stay here anymore.

Larry survived two very savage assaults on his person by the devil, yet he lived for two years and never experienced another cardiac arrest. The odds against that happening are so astronomical that they actually support divine intervention as the proximate cause and therefore rules out "chance" as even a remote possibility.

So, Larry died anyway. If he was receiving all of that divine intervention to keep him alive and to keep him coherent, then why didn't God just go all the way and instantly heal him like we were expecting?

Here is one impression that I have received from God; "Because people soon forget miracles, (just look at the Israelites) but I have been able to bring you and many others on a journey of spiritual growth through Larry's experience." So the journey continues.

"Reflect upon your present blessings, of which every man has plenty; not on your past misfortunes, of which all men have some." ~Charles Dickens

A friend wrote in a card, "We have no words. The two of you fought so hard." Truly the last words in Larry's heart were, *"I have fought the good fight, I have finished the race, I have kept the faith."* (2 Timothy 4:7)

Joyfully His,
Stacie

November 18, 2009
Subject: Just Wondering...

Hello Everyone,

I was given this profound thought during my prayer time this morning: DEATH IS TEMPORARY - LIFE IS ETERNAL.

"Gratitude unlocks the fullness of life. It turns what we have into enough, and more. It turns denial into acceptance, chaos into order, and confusion to clarity. It can turn a meal into a feast, a house into a home, a stranger into a friend. Gratitude makes sense of our past, brings peace for today, and creates a vision for tomorrow." ~Melody Beattie, author of "May You Be Blessed"

I will be helping Matthew's father install his headstone on Saturday. It makes me wonder what other things that we may collaborate on in the future that will be a blessing to others.

Some of you believe me to be stoic or brave. The truth is that I have a gift for compartmentalization, and there is only one being big enough to withstand the maelstrom of my anguish. Therefore, I do not burden the rest of you with my ranting's.

Joyfully His,

Stacie

P.S. I am on the precipice of a whole new epic adventure in my life, and I must be sure it is God's voice that I am seeking and not what I think or what well meaning friends think I should be doing.

November 25, 2009
Subject: Happy Thanksgiving

Hello Everyone,

I cannot adequately express how blessed and thankful that I am to all of you for your years of love, patience, kindness and service to me and my family. I am overwhelmed with tears of joy and gratefulness at your compassion. You have all been so good to me. Thank you!

Today marks one month since Larry died and two and a half months for Matthew. Yes, I am pining for them something awful, but I choose to dawn my rose-colored glasses and visualize Heaven and them doing the things that bring them the most pleasure. To me they are not dead. Their bodies have ceased to function in this dimension of existence, but they live on for all eternity with Jesus.

"We determine whether something will be a blessing or a curse by the way we choose to see it." ~Kate Nowak

"Life's most persistent and urgent question is: What are you doing for others?" ~ Martin Luther King, Jr.

"What lies behind us, and what lies before us are small matters compared to what lies within us." ~ Ralph Waldo Emerson

Although it may seem counter intuitive; I am choosing to be thankful for all that I have. I am thankful for those things that are truly important, and that does not include possessions.

I love you sooooooooooooo much,
Stacie

December 24, 2009
Subject: Merry Christmas

Hi Everybody,

I am so grateful to know that I have friends that I can truly count on and that each of you know that you can truly count upon me. I wouldn't trade these relationships for anything. Relationships are actually all that we have, and they are the only things that are of eternal significance. Our love and memory of one another and our relationship with God is everlasting. Jesus came as a helpless little baby, just like each of us, and grew just like each of us, so that He could have a personal relationship, just with each of us.

I love you so much and pray that our relationships grow stronger in 2010.

Joyfully His,
Stacie

Chapter 7

ॐ

February 6, 2010
Subject: A New Perspective

Hello Everyone,

S orry that I have not written to you in quite a while. It is a little hard to describe, but it is like walking around in a thick fog taking the same number of steps in the same direction as you always have, but it doesn't feel like you are going through the motions. I have had some happy moments and some very sad ones as well. A friend likened the events during the last three years of my life to urban combat and some of my symptoms to post traumatic stress syndrome, but I promise not to go postal on anyone. I do not know how long this healing process is going to take but, the operative word here is PROCESS. Every process takes time and this one does not have a definitive timetable with predictable interim goals. I am eager to find my new happy place, but until I do, please continue to pray for me to remain glued to the only One that can lead me through this process.

Yesterday, I attended a Change of Command Ceremony on the aircraft carrier, USS Harry S. Truman, for the air wing commanders. I was intrigued by the fact that both commanders quoted the same man without previously conferring about their speeches. I do not believe in luck or coincidence, so I took this saying to heart. "I am exactly where I want to be, doing exactly what I want to do." Isn't that a powerful statement? I used to say the same thing when I was in the military along with the fact that I couldn't believe that they were actually paying me to have that much fun! I thought back to the last time I said that same thing and was suddenly enlightened. The reason that these men are able to make such a bodacious statement is because they are both where they are supposed to be, doing exactly what they are suppose to be doing. This brings me to the profound conclusion that no one can be happy or satisfied being or doing something that they are not SUPPOSED to be or do.

So how do I reconcile my life in light of this philosophy for what I am supposed to do? The only perceived choice I had in controlling anything during the last three years was in whether I would desert Larry or devote myself to him with a titanium strength resolve. But even that choice was a no brainer for me. Did I do something or fail to do something that caused these events in my life? Is there anything that I could have done differently that would have changed the outcome; meaning to prevent Matthew or Larry's death? No. So am I not exactly where I am supposed to be, doing exactly what I am supposed to be doing? If you are not exactly where you want to be, doing exactly what you want to be doing, then where are you SUPPOSED to be?

A really fabulous book to help you align your priorities is "The Purpose Driven Life" by Rick Warren. It could just as easily be titled, "What Am I SUPPOSED To Be Doing With My Life?"

I am currently writing a book and starting two companies, because that is exactly where I want to be, doing exactly what I want to do, because that is exactly what I am supposed to do!

I am convinced and sure that He who began a good work in you will continue it until the day of Jesus Christ, devel-

oping and perfecting and bringing it into full completion in you. (Philippians 1:6) This has become my favorite scripture for summarizing my life's journey.

Joyfully His,
Stacie

June 10, 2010
Subject: Life Update

Hello Everybody,

It has been a long time since I wrote an update, so here it goes...

I have been doing a lot of hard work processing through the healing process and some days I am just plum bipolar! I never know when a thought or emotion or situation is going to trigger a response, and it is like being ambushed by my emotions. Thankfully, I haven't had it happen very often when around strangers. Today marks nine months since Matthew went to Heaven; seven months since Larry went home to be with the Lord and it just seems like yesterday to me.

Recently I was able to attend a bio-ethics symposium at Regent University that really brought into focus some things that Larry and I encountered during his diminished state. We dodged at least four bullets in the process of his illness. Our country is truly on the precipice of ruling on the worthiness of each life's value regardless of that person's desire or the desire of their family members. Everything is motivated by money. A persons' value and eligibility to receive care will depend upon a predetermined formula of worthiness.

My life's mission is to help many people walk through the storms in their lives with courage, dignity and unstoppable faith. Every human being on this planet goes through a storm at some point in their lives, maybe even multiple times. Those storms are going to hurt like crazy, but there is joy in the morning if you know the secret.

I just cannot adequately express how much I love and appreciate each of you. I am so grateful for your love, kindness, patience and long-suffering with me. There is just no substitute for brotherly kindness or brotherly (or sisterly) love. God sure knew what he was doing when he put us all together didn't He?

Joyfully His,
Stacie

July 6, 2010
Subject: Some Personal Revelations

Hello Everyone,

Each day has its own purpose! Each day is a day the Lord has made for a specific purpose. No matter the circumstances or how I feel about them, each day has a purpose! We cannot skip a day or put them in a different order. I have tried to skip a few by just pulling the covers over my head all day, but the day still exists whether I want to acknowledge it or not. It is so amazing to realize that each day and every infinitesimal detail existing in it all have a specific role in completing that day. No matter how wonderful or horrific your day has been, take a step back and view it from the perspective of purpose: how it affects you, your family, your country or planet and use that information to make tomorrow better.

So when the storm is upon you, remember that God, like a trainer of fine warriors, has matched you against a formidable and stalwart antagonist. All God's children face challenges. That is how we grow and overcome to become what God has destined us to be. Overcoming challenges is a natural part of the maturing process for any organism. The great beauty in what God orchestrates on our behalf is that He allows us to be pitted against an enemy that we are only able to overcome with His help, thus maximizing the necessity to stretch ourselves in faith and therefore strengthening our relationship with Him. Remember, it is IMPOSSIBLE to please God without faith.

People who are hurting have a tendency to hurt other people. During the past three years, I have said many things to people that may have lacked sensitivity in delivery, though I have never intentionally hurt anyone, but that certainly does not account for the manner in which my comments were received. One possible explanation is that in my focus on coping with the tragedies in my own life I have accidentally and unknowingly stomped on a raw nerve in someone else's world. You never know what affect your words may have on another, either for positive or negative since you cannot see their background.

Life is all about choices. When you cut away all the junk, every situation is a choice. You choose how you react to situations. You choose how you will allow people to affect your mood. You choose to be in a good mood or bad mood. The bottom line: It's your choice how you live your life.

Wow, I know that this is a pretty heavy e-mail but I pray that it inspires each of us to keep our lives in perspective and live abundantly every day.

Joyfully His,
Stacie

July 7, 2010
Subject: Some Pearls of Wisdom

Hi Everybody,

"What you leave behind is not what is engraved in stone monuments, but what is woven into the lives of others." ~Pericles

"Many people die with their music still in them. Why is this so? Too often it is because they are always getting ready to live. Before they know it, time runs out." ~ Oliver Wendell Holmes, Jr.

"By wisdom a house is built, through understanding it is established; a wise man has great power and a man of knowledge increases strength; for waging war you need guidance, and for victory many advisers." (Proverbs 24:3-5) All the sons of God are waging war against an unseen enemy that is often able to manifest itself through the actions of people as well as in catastrophes.

We rejoice in the glory of God. And not only that, but we also glory in our tribulations, knowing that tribulation produces perseverance; and perseverance, character; and character, hope. Now hope does not disappoint, because the love of God has been poured out in our hearts by the Holy Spirit who was given to us. (Romans 5:2-5) We live in treacherous times and God's enemy is our enemy.

Live simply, love generously, care deeply, speak kindly and leave the rest to God!

"Resolve to be tender with the young, compassionate with the aged, sympathetic with the striving, and tolerant with the weak... because in your life you will have been all of these." ~ Mac Anderson

"Courage is what it takes to stand up and speak; courage is also what it takes to sit down and listen." ~ Winston Churchill

"There once was a very cautious man, who never laughed or cried, he never cared, he never dared, he never dreamed or tried. And when one day he passed away, his insurance was denied. For since he never really lived, they claimed he never died." ~ Tom Mathews

"A single sunbeam is enough to drive away many shadows." ~ St. Francis of Assisi

"Wisdom outweighs any wealth." ~ Sophocles

"Though no one can go back and make a brand new start, anyone can start from now and make a brand new ending." ~ Carl Bard

Finally, my friends, whatever is true, whatever is honest, whatever is right, whatever is pure, whatever is lovely, whatever is admirable, if anything is excellent or praiseworthy, think about these things. (Philippians 4:8) God's wisdom even tells us how to guide our minds to keep ourselves on track.

We all have vast amounts of knowledge stored in our random access memory banks, regardless of whether we obtained it through books, experience or even instinct. Knowledge without action is just trivia, the same as faith without corresponding works is worthless. Wisdom is when you apply the knowledge obtained to produce a beneficial result.

As the children of God, we are called to imitate our Creator. As Christ followers we have the perfect image to reflect in our lives. There is no greater wisdom or higher calling to emulate than that of Jesus the Messiah.

Living wisely produces love, joy, peace, patience, goodness, kindness, gentleness, faithfulness and self-discipline. You probably recognize these traits as the fruit of the Spirit. Applying these attributes in our lives is not only wise but awesomely beneficial to us as well as to all who come into contact with us. What an enjoyable and fulfilling life each of us could have if we merely concentrated on living wisely.

I pray that each of us has the tenacity to act wisely in these last days and to walk in fruitful bliss. Think of how many lives can be positively impacted by your decision.

Joyfully His,
Stacie

July 12, 2010
Subject: Joy?

Hello My Dear Friends,

"Life does not cease to be funny when people die any more than it ceases to be serious when people laugh." ~ George Bernard Shaw

"The walls we build around us to keep sadness out also keeps out the joy." ~ Jim Rohn

It is written that the joy of the Lord is our true source of strength. It seems inconceivable or at the very least counterintuitive to experience joy in a midst of personal devastation. Let's be real! It is during our most catastrophic events such as terrorist attacks, tsunamis, earthquakes, floods, hurricanes, drought, wars, fires and even a collision with Wormwood (as mentioned in Rev. 8:11) that we require the most emotional, intellectual and physical strength. How ironic it is to think that the source of our strength is hidden in something that is the furthest thing from our minds in a crisis?

Today marks three years since Larry and I heard Dr. Lawson diagnose him with leukemia. I had such a sick feeling in my gut yesterday that it prevented me from slapping on my happy face and marching off to church like a good little soldier.

So what is the big difference between happiness and joy? Happiness is a temporary sensation, but joy is an eternal experience. The joy of knowing that this life is just a temporary proving ground and that I will spend all eternity with my loving Father gives me unfathomable strength to overcome any circumstance.

My all time favorite scripture is Philippians 4:8 because it is like Jesus giving me specific instructions on how to stay on course in order to accomplish my life's mission. *Finally, my friends, whatever things are true, whatever things are honest, whatever things are just, whatever things are pure, whatever things are lovely, whatever things are of good report; if there be any virtue, and if anything is praiseworthy, THINK ON THESE THINGS.*

With the many pressures of life, it's important that we have a lighthearted attitude towards any situation that tries to steal our joy. We must remember to focus on the One who has called us out of darkness and into His marvelous light. Having a lighthearted and cheerful attitude not only helps to keep our joy, but it also helps to restore our health. *A cheerful heart is good like a medicine: but a broken spirit dries up the bones.* (Proverbs 17:22). Have a merry heart and do not allow the pressures of the enemy to steal your joy and make you question your destiny. Stand steadfast in your faith and make up your mind that your joy will continue all the days of your life.

Be encouraged to not be so serious all the time. If you are finding yourself having a bad day, stop yourself and think on Philippians 4:8, maybe even speak it out loud to adjust your attitude. It is our choice whether we react in peace and joy or bitterness and unforgiveness. Put a smile on your lips and know in your heart that the Lord has done all the work for you to eternally live with Him in joy.

Joyfully His,
Stacie

July 23, 2010
Subject: Repentance

Hello Everyone,

Repentance by definition is to feel sorry, self reproachful, or contrite for a past action, attitude or thoughtless act; to feel remorse for sin or fault; to feel sorry for or to regret.

In all that my family has endured in the past years part of my soul feels great penitence for acts of omission and commission both premeditated and out of ignorance. It is no small wonder that the grieving process can take many years to unravel.

God has specifically hardwired our souls for repentance for the express purpose of using our own freewill to make a change in our behavior for the future. I can beat myself up relentlessly and feel guilty as sin for the past, but I cannot affect it in the least millisecond. I can however allow the past to either be my friend or my foe. If I choose to beat myself up, filled with anguish over the "what if" questions, and fail to take responsibility for my own actions then I will be destined to stew in endless torturous venom with zero hope. But God has provided a way out of that dead end ambush if we will merely release our guilt, regrets and wrong doings to Him.

Repentance is actually considered a precious sacrament by the Catholics and really it is the only release we have from the treacherous trap Satan has set for each of us. It is only through repentance that we can receive forgiveness, even if the wronged party can no longer forgive you, you can be forgiven and not repeat the same behavior in the future toward others.

Repentance is truly a very freeing experience. We are just imperfect people doing our best. In trying to carry all of our mistakes around with us, we become so burdened, stressed and depressed that it becomes impossible for us to function as our Creator intended.

Many years ago just after I turned my life over to Jesus, I felt the need to do penance for my past wrongs by trying to help others. I can never go back and right the wrongs, but I can repent of my actions and resolve to change my future behavior. I know that the word penance carries a negative connotation, but actually it can be very rewarding when done to honor God or for the benefit of others.

Yes, this has been a rather somber email but without repentance there can be no forgiveness, leaving us hopelessly doomed for all eternity, not just miserable here and now.

Many years ago a wise person told me that the best medicine for depression or the perfect cure for insurmountable problems was to take my eyes off of myself and to focus on others. Perhaps that is what true repentance and penance is all about.

Joyfully His,
Stacie

August 23, 2010
Subject: A Sacrifice of Praise

Hello Everyone,

I am feeling apprehensive about the first anniversary of Matthew's death on September 10th. I have been somewhat overwhelmed with emotions. Sometimes I cannot even believe that it is true, let alone that it happened almost a year ago? There is still so much to process, clean up and repair in terms of relationships in the aftermath of this storm.

When I turned my life over to Jesus in 1994, I did not understand the term in scripture that commands us to offer up to God a sacrifice of praise. Really, how in the world could praising the God that I love and adore be a sacrifice? After all, I pledged with my whole heart to imitate His only begotten Son in all my actions. How could praise ever require a sacrifice since it is just as easy and natural as falling off of a log? A sacrifice would mean that it cost me something, but it would also mean that I gave it willingly because it was the right thing to do. Now, however, I comprehend the full magnitude of what a critically powerful key praise is in the spiritual realm. I personally know what it costs to choose to honor, trust and praise God even though I know He could have spared all of us from years of suffering.

There is a scripture that states that God knew the number of my days before I was even conceived. Though I can't begin to understand why He allows horrible catastrophic things to happen in this world (even to His chosen people), I know for a fact that He loves and adores us. I choose to respond to His love by cheerfully giving Him my heart in a sacrifice of praise, song, thanksgiving and adoration regardless of the storm He has asked me to endure.

During the paste three years I have spent a great deal of time studying one of God's champions and my hero,

Job, in the book of Job. I have always been amazed at how God asked Satan if he had noticed His servant Job and literally provoked Satan to terrorize Job. After Satan had been allowed to destroy all of Job's ships, cattle, flocks, servants, property and all 10 of his children, Job, my hero reacted in the most powerful act of love and honor that anyone has ever heard of. Job fell to the ground and worshipped God then said, "May the name of the Lord be praised!" In all this, Job did not sin by charging God with wrongdoing! Then Job asked, "Shall we accept good from God, and not trouble?" In all of this, Job did not sin in what he said.

That kind of reaction is just not humanly possible without some kind of supernatural empowerment; so... where did he get it? Praise is a dynamically powerful key to faith. Praise is the secret ingredient to expressing our faith, hope and love toward our Creator! Praise is the catalytic molecule that unites all the working parts. Praise is the critical missing link that will allow the restoration of God to manifest in our lives.

As Job neared the end of his ordeal the Lord answered Job out of the storm (Job 38:1) and then the Lord spoke to Job out of the storm (Job 40:6) It is fascinating that God communicated directly to Job twice in the midst of his storm, but not until he had proved himself faithful and exactly as God had portrayed him to Satan in the first place.

There are a couple of songs that I have heard recently that have really ministered to me in a wonderful way. They are: "Praise You in the Storm" and "When Praise Demands a Sacrifice." Some of the lyrics to the latter song are "when praise demands a sacrifice I will worship even then, surrendering the dearest things in life. If my devotion costs it all, I will be faithful no matter the circumstances."

God doesn't want our praise, because He thinks He is hot stuff and just wants to lord His magnificence over us! No, He loves and adores each of us unconditionally. God only wants good for us and will provide opportunities to bring out the best in us if we will allow Him. Most of us will never personally experience what Job endured, but exercising praise is truly the answer to weathering any storm.

Hidden in each one of you is the powerful faith to be a champion for God by overcoming any situation with love, praise and worship. It is a supernatural power house combination that will subdue all the fears that the enemy brings against you. Praise is the critical missing link to fulfilling your destiny. I plan to sling it like a battle axe every time my thoughts are assailed by grief or overwhelming emotions.

Joyfully His,
Stacie

August 30, 2010
Subject: Attitude of Gratitude

Hi Everybody,

Gratitude may very well define a successful life. Being grateful is akin to seeing the glass as half full. Choosing to count your blessings rather than wallowing in self absorption or lusting after people or things is truly choosing the higher ground that will pay priceless eternal dividends.

Five days ago marked 10 months since my sweet Larry died and this Friday will be our 17th wedding anniversary. I shudder to think about where I would be right now if I didn't have an anchor securely fastened to the very core of creation. I would have been dashed to pieces on the rocks of self-destruction long ago. No human being can withstand the constant pummeling of concurrent hurricanes alone. Even if your body somehow managed to survive your mind would snap. That is exactly why water-boarding (no pun intended) is such an effective torture.

"Keep company with those who make you better, not bitter."
~ Old English Proverb

"As we express our gratitude, we must never forget that the highest appreciation is not to utter words, but to live by them." ~ John Fitzgerald Kennedy

"There's a special kind of magic in gratitude that raises our consciousness to see just how small we are in the cosmos. If pride is the root of all sin in the universe, and it is, then gratitude is the cure as well as the salve of humility." ~ Author Unknown

"Gratitude is not a fair weather virtue. True gratitude means appreciating your life no matter what the storms may bring. Is simply being alive gift enough for you to feel grateful?" ~ Mac Anderson, author of "Learning to Dance in the Rain"

While looking back at my life I realize just how many loved ones I have out lived. My maternal grandparents, mother, father, a cousin, five brothers-in-law, two sisters-in-law, a niece, a nephew, my husband, my only child and numerous dear friends. As horrible as each of their passing was to me, it dims in comparison to the millions who did not survive the Holocaust, 9/11, Katrina, Haiti, famines, earthquakes, wars and tsunamis who have no hope of meeting up with their loved ones in eternity. I am so grateful to have understood that not only can I have a personal relationship with The Almighty, but that He actually wants to be my friend. I am so grateful to understand that this existence is just a temporary journey as a proving ground for the human spirit and that God has things planned for eternity that we cannot even begin to imagine. I am so grateful for all of the human spirits that God has allowed me to love and traverse this planet with during my life span. I am so grateful to know the one true and living God and to know that He loves me as much as He loves His own Son. I am so grateful that God has chosen us to bravely share His love in a lost, depraved, hopeless and frightened world.

I assure you that there is no tragedy in your life that you will have to face alone. Your Creator has designed you with the capacity to soar up above the clouds like an eagle and gratefully ride out the storms that will come in your life. God has promised to never leave you. Any disaster is survivable when you gratefully acknowledge the One who created everything seen and unseen.

Joyfully His,
Stacie

September 6, 2010
Subject: The Curse of Unforgiveness

Hi Everybody,

Like anyone else on this planet I have numerous cuts, bruises and broken parts in varying levels of healing at any given point in time. Some of my hurts are self-inflicted. But, the most grievous sorrow that I could ever bring upon myself is the CURSE of UNFORGIVENESS.

The most beautiful example of divine intervention concerning forgiveness that I know about is encapsulated in the testimony of Joyce Meyers. Her own father sexually abused her for years right under her mother's nose. She was mentally, physically and emotionally devastated in the most cruel torture imaginable! I encourage each of you to check out her story on the web. What a miracle transformation of God it is to see her whole and ministering to millions of people worldwide.

Isn't it interesting to see how the people dearest to us can push our buttons beyond our ability to control ourselves? Why is it that we often speak more harshly to our family than to anyone else? Sometimes we say cutting things that pack a more powerful punch than any weapon ever could. Instead of slugging a person, we hit them in the heart with our words delivering irreparable damage. A bruise will heal in a few days, but a wounded spirit will fester and fester until someone reaches in there with the love of God to heal it.

"Forgiveness is almost a selfish act because of its immense benefits to the one who forgives." ~ Lawana Blackwell, Leaving the Pain Behind

"Have you ever tried to forgive someone and found you simply couldn't do it? You've cried about it and prayed about it and asked God to help you, but those old feelings of resentment just failed to go away? You can put an end to those kinds of failures in the future by basing your forgiveness on faith rather than feelings. True forgiveness doesn't have anything at all to do with how you feel. It's an act of your will. It is based on obedience to God and on faith in Him. That means once you've forgiven a person, you need to consider him or her permanently forgiven! When old feelings rise up within you and Satan tries to convince you that you haven't really forgiven, resist him. Say, "No, I've already forgiven that person by faith. I refuse to dwell on those old feelings." Then, according to 1 John 1:9, believe that you receive forgiveness and cleansing from the sin of unforgiveness and from all unrighteousness associated with it including any remembrance of having been wronged!" ~ Brother Copeland

"Have you ever heard anyone say, "I may forgive, but I'll never forget!" That's a second-rate kind of forgiveness that you, as a believer, are never supposed to settle for. You're to forgive supernaturally, *even as God for Christ's sake has forgiven you*. (Ephesians 4:32) You're to forgive as God forgives. To release that person from guilt permanently and unconditionally and to operate as if nothing bad ever happened between you. You're to purposely forget as well as forgive. As you do that, something supernatural will happen within you. The pain once caused by that incident will disappear. The power of God will wash away the effects of it and you'll be able to leave it behind you once and for all." ~ Brother Copeland

Don't become an emotional bookkeeper, keeping careful accounts of the wrongs you have suffered. Learn to forgive and forget. It will open a whole new world of blessing for you. It really helps me to read Luke 6:27-37.

"When you play it too safe, you're taking the biggest risk of your life...Time is the only wealth we're given." ~ Barbara Sher

I refuse to waist my precious time, energy and life being hurt, angry or holding a grudge against anyone, especially against myself for some of the stupid things that I have done in my past. Really, if you have repented for some senseless or premeditated act, then Jesus is faithful to forgive you and cast the offense into a sea of forgetfulness. Who in the world do you think you are that you are so important as to hold it against yourself? For those of us living in the U.S. with unlimited freedom and privilege, it is only the enemy that wants you to waste your life in self-recrimination and depression!

It is a proven medical fact that holding a grudge will corrupt your health, eating you alive as surely as cancer. Perhaps there is a correlation. But the number one reason for letting go and forgiving is because Jesus said to forgive. *And when you stand praying, if you hold anything against anyone, forgive him, so that your Father in heaven may forgive your sins.* (Mark 11:25)

Joyfully His,
Stacie

September 10, 2010
Subject: Extravagant Love

Hello Everybody,

Maybe Love Really Does Conqueror All...
What do I know about love? What does anyone know about love? Only God, who is love, can possibly answer that question.

Today marks exactly one year since my only child, Matthew, died. Where is the love in that? How do I know what love is? Well at least one aspect of love is based upon how badly you miss a person when you are apart from them for any time. Then another is how you feel about them and yourself when you are together. Still another aspect of love is your willingness to sacrifice your desires for those of another.

Some intimate journal entries to my God:

Many years ago I promised that I would follow You wherever You led me. I

I promised that even if You asked the impossible from me that I would refuse You nothing. My concept of refusing You nothing in my life naturally did not include my son or my husband. Lord, now I ask You to help me follow You when I do not have the strength or the desire to move forward. Help me to trust you as much as I long to love You.

Thank You for faithfully reassuring me with your promises Lord that following You will be more than worth the pain.

You know that I love You Lord because I relinquish my will to You. You have the right to choose for me anything that You please.

Here I am Lord empty and deserted waiting on You to fill me to overflowing with Your love.

My God, You are right and pure and just. I can depend upon You to never change; thus You remain perfect.

Lord, I believe that all of these painful experiences are somehow being used for my good to make me stronger in relying upon You to prepare me for the ultimate sacrifice. After all, I was all gung-ho and willing to give my life for my country as a soldier, but now I have promised to give my life for You.

Dear Jesus, it is your voice I love to hear and joyfully obey.

"Be of good cheer my love, it is I, don't be afraid." ~ Jesus.

I have been hemmed in on all sides; there really is only one logical path for me to follow. I have been put in a position where there is nothing to interfere with our relationship, nothing to distract me from You.

Thank You God for developing and training me in Your word so I will not compromise my faith in You. Now I am sure that there is no way that I would ever renounce You to follow the Anti-Christ.

As I look at the life of Corrie ten Boom I realize that she was only doing good and she was certainly in Your will Lord, yet You allowed her family to be caught, tortured and imprisoned in a Nazi concentration camp. Her family died for their beliefs! ~ Grow me, discipline me, and train me to be that kind of warrior in Your Army Lord.

God, You have shown me great love and mercy by not discarding me when I turned my back on You, living a life of absolute infamy. I don't know how You put up with me except for love!

Discipline, sacrifice and courage are acts of love.

I love You enough to trust You completely. As much as I love You and trust You now, I ask You to guide me and teach me to love You still more. I cannot continue to exist without loving You.

Help me Lord to only strike back at my enemies with love.

Love is the ultimate sacrifice. No matter how hard, lonely or cruel my life seems, please don't let me turn from You my love.

Yes, Lord I will still trust and love You no matter what You ask of me. No matter what happens because I know that You have personally prepared me and are in me through everything You ask me to face. I am Your vessel, Your temple, Your dwelling place.

Jesus, do not urge me to leave You or turn back from following you. Where You go I will go. Where You stay I will stay. Your people will be my people and Your God my God. (Adapted from Ruth 1:6)

I love you Jesus. I don't just seek the rewards that you have promised - I seek to be with you, doing what you are doing. Jesus I want YOU! NOTHING else matters to me but to be with you Jesus!

Love is beautiful, but it is also terrible. Terrible because of its determination to allow nothing blemished or unworthy to remain in the beloved. Jesus, because you love me, I willingly give you every spot and blemish to cleanse. I am convinced and sure that He who began a good work in me will continue until the day of Christ Jesus, developing and perfecting and bringing it into full completion in me. (Philippians 1:6)

Love is alive with great joy in my heart so that I utterly abandon myself to the ecstasy of giving it to others. To cast my will down in love, surrender and obedience to Jesus as my greatest joy!

Eternal life in love with Jesus is reality, it is this physical life that is the illusion.

God's love is reality whether I comprehend it or not. The work He is doing in me is perfecting my love for Him as I have so earnestly requested.

I have been crucified with Christ. It is no longer I who lives but Christ lives in me and the life that I now live in the flesh, I live by faith in the Son of God who loved me and gave his life for me. (Galatians 2:20) I no longer desire to live for my own desires but only for you Jesus.

Behold, I have set My love upon you and you are Mine... yes, I have loved you with an everlasting love: therefore with loving-kindness I have drawn you to Me. ~ God

God, teach me to see others as You see them. Teach me to love mankind as You love us.

There is no circumstance in life, no matter how wicked or ugly it appears to be, if it is reacted to in love, forgiveness and obedience to Your will that cannot be transformed. I resolve to overcome evil with good, by applying Your love to every situation.

A conqueror merely overcomes his opponent by force, but I am more than a conqueror, because I overcome evil by the force of LOVE. (End of journal rambling)

In all the world only one thing really matters; to do the will of the One that you profess to love, no matter what is involved or the cost.

I love all of you dearly,

Stacie

September 27, 2010
Subject: Some Encouragement...

Hello my Dear Friends,

"We sometimes feel that what we do is just a drop in the ocean, but the ocean would be less because of that missing drop." ~ Mother Teresa

"We are continually faced with insolvable problems brilliantly disguised as great opportunities." ~ Larry Ebinger

"When difficult times come our way and we feel tempted to lose our peace, we must remember that God is still in control and holds us securely in the palms of His hands. His strength is what should keep us strong and confident in His ability and remind us that in His sight All Is Well. Do not allow the enemy to steal the Joy that is in your heart, but rather stand steadfast in your faith knowing that if God be for you, who can dare to be against you? The Bible says that He keeps you as the apple of His eye and has carved you upon the palms of His hands. Such love cannot be understood, yet exists without question to all who will simply receive it." ~ Don Savaya

"More people fail for lack of encouragement, than for any other reason." ~Ruth Graham Bell

"Never let a single day pass without saying an encouraging word to each child." ~Paula J. Fox, "Heart of a Teacher"

"When one door closes another one opens. What you believe is the worst moment of your life could turn out to be the beginning of a new and better life..." ~ Margie Tsoukias

"Character cannot be developed in ease and quiet. Only through experience of trial and suffering can the soul be strengthened, vision cleared, ambition inspired, and success achieved." ~ Hellen Keller,

Never allow the enemy's intended discouragement make you question your abilities. Be Strong in the Lord and in the power of His Might. Do not allow yourself to question if you are able to overcome the obstacles that come before you, but rather be reassured and know that the qualities that God has placed within you are more than sufficient to overcome and be triumphant over every trial that comes your way. (Ephesians 6:10-14)

"Do not wait; the time will never be 'just right.' Start where you stand, and work with whatever tools you may have at your command, and better tools will be found as you go along." ~ Napoleon Hill

"Every single thing you do matters. You have been created as one of a kind. You have been created in order to make a difference. You have within you the power to change the world." ~ Andy Andrews

"Courage is fear that has said its prayers." ~ Dorothy Bernard

"Be encouraged to not be so serious all the time. If you are finding yourself having a bad day, stop yourself and think on something good or funny. Have a merry heart and keep it in your mind that it is for your own best interest to take it easy and enjoy right now. The Bible declares in Proverbs 15:13:

A merry heart maketh a cheerful countenance: but by sorrow of the heart the spirit is broken. It is our choice whether we have peace and joy or heartbreak and disappointment. The Lord has done all the work that needed to be done and now it is up to us whether we accept it or reject it." ~ Don Savaya

I encourage each of you to see the good in all things and do not allow the voice of discouragement to penetrate your heart. Have a merry heart and allow God's peace to infiltrate every area of your life. You will find very soon if you choose to have a merry heart that your health, joy, contentment and peace will be elevated to heights never before imagined.

Joyfully His,
Stacie

October 29, 2010
Subject: Life Today

Hello Everyone,

This is a very significant day in history for us. Three years ago today Larry passed out in our kitchen, died and was resurrected. One year ago today we buried him. Has it really been that long? Where has my life gone? Where am I going? What am I suppose to be doing?

I guess today has really been marked as a kind of spiritual gut check. For so many years Larry and I walked hand in hand in unadulterated childlike faith, knowing that God loved us with all of His heart and that He is a good father that will never leave or forsake us. Of course neither of us could have ever anticipated what would come to pass in the circumstances of our lives. Part of us still operated under somewhat of a fairytale dilution that because we were believers that our God would never let anything bad happen in our lives. That sounds so incredibly stupid and immature to me but I would be willing to bet that we were not alone in that way of thinking.

While observing all of the greatest faith heroes in the Bible it is very evident that those who suffered the most while maintaining their faith in the God of Abraham, Isaac and Jacob were the biggest victors! Those are the people of great renown, not the people who never had any challenges. We don't admire someone for what he has accomplished if there was no personal price paid. We don't respect someone just because they have talent or high intelligence unless they are using that gift to benefit others, particularly in a sacrificial way.

In retrospect I can clearly see how our faith evolved as we grew in our relationship with the One who made the promises that we believed. Here is how faith and wishful thinking diverge: faith is believing the promise that God is always with you and will always keep you even through the deadliest storm, shipwreck or beating; the illusion is thinking that you will never face challenges. My God is an awesome God. He is yearning for His children to stand up under pressure and forcefully trust Him to lead them in any situation. Jesus is knocking at the door of your heart. Let him in so he can prove his faithfulness and power to you personally. Jesus sacrificed his whole life because of his ardent love for you. He is asking for your trust in return.

I would like to encourage you to breathe this one line prayer several times each day. ~ "Lord, give me a life that will make a difference forever, not a comfortable life."

Forever joyfully His,
Stacie

Epilogue

❧❧

We were all created as triune creatures, spirit soul, and body. In our body it is easy to understand the cause and effect of input verses output and exercise. Our soul which is comprised by our mind, will and emotions, operates the same way. If we fail to keep our mind sharp with mental calisthenics the neuropathways fade with apathy just like our muscles without exercise. However, the most important aspect of our being from which we derive all life is also the eternal portion. How do we exercise that part of our being? The answer is through two-way communication with our Creator and meditation on His Word.

The saying," if you don't use it you will lose it." is so simplistic, accurate and vital to every aspect of our being! There is no possible way for me to have survived the catastrophic losses in my life with any shred of sanity without a deep abiding relationship with our Creator. Only with God could I negotiate these tragedies and actually come out better, stronger, more alive, compassionate and willing to give generously into the lives of other devastated people.

You may ask; how can you get started on a path to spiritual unity with the Creator? There is no preordained formula to follow. I can only share with you how I did it and encourage you to develop your own path.

One Sunday morning in 1994 I attended an interdenominational service as part of a business convention. The speaker was just an ordinary man that asked a series of thought provoking questions which made me seriously evaluate my purpose for existing.

He started by sharing his antics in college and numerous encounters with chemicals which I could identify with. He talked about how he had succumbed to peer and social pressures to be accepted even though he had to compromise what he knew was right in order to fit in. He shared how he had clearly done things that were illegal because they were fun to do. I certainly knew where he was coming from.

Suddenly the course of his questions and hilarious adventures shifted when he asked, "If you were killed in a car accident on your way home today would you go to Heaven?

I thought to myself, "Well who could ever know that for sure?"

He asked, "If I could show you a way that you could be sure that you would go to Heaven if you died today, would you want to know?"

I thought to myself, "Well, duh, who wouldn't want to know that?"

He went on to explain that by our own admission we had all sinned and were separated from God through our willful or ignorant disobedience. He said that because God is our loving Father and Creator, and He wants to forgive our sins, all we need to do is ask. God loves us and wants a relationship with us more than we do. He then explained how we became separated from God in the first place and how His Son Jesus died a physical sacrificial death in our place as a consequence of our sin so that we could be reconciled to God. God had sacrificed His only begotten son on our behalf just so we could be reconciled in our relationship with Him and therefore the only way to accept this free absolution is through the blood of Jesus.

He then asked, "Do you believe that Jesus is the Son of God?"

Well to me that was a no-brainer, of course Jesus is the Son of God and I knew he died for me, but now I actually understood the connection. Yes, I was 38 years old and never actually knew how one affected the other until that moment!

Again I was thinking to myself, "This is so simple and clear. There is no way God could make this any easier!"

Finally this man said that if I confess with my voice the Lord Jesus and believe in my heart that God raised him from the dead that I would be saved and Jesus would proclaim me as his throughout all the heavens and all eternity!

I nearly exploded with excitement! I was thinking: "Do you mean to tell me that all I have to do to be sure of my eternal life in Heaven is to proclaim what I already know in my heart to be true? Really? You must be joking. God has done all the work, paid the price, suffered thousands of years and all I have to do is say yes to what He wants to lavish upon me? I would have to be out of my mind to refuse such a magnificent gift! So how do I do this?"

The man sweetly invited anyone who wished to proclaim Jesus as Lord over their life and receive eternal life to come down to the front of the coliseum. I don't remember now if I ran or not but I was sitting in the back balcony of huge building and I was the first to reach the stage in my exuberance.

I gave my life to Jesus that day to use me anyway he saw fit. I had made a mess of my life so I knew he couldn't do any worse but most of all I was hoping to live a life that would be pleasing to God.

It has been 18 months since my son and husband died yet God has truly brought me through this ordeal to a sweeter relationship with Him than I could have ever imagined. His love and faithfulness is more beautiful than anything on the planet. God has in fact extracted the greatest amount of good out of the most vile of circumstances. In God's system of justice (just as in physics) there is a consequence to every action. There is a just reward for every deed whether good or bad. I am an eternal being having a temporary experience that my Father will weigh in His balance and settle all scores.

There is absolutely no storm that can ever overwhelm you when you are sure of your perfect Father's love and devotion for all eternity.

Joyfully His for all eternity,
Stacie